Quadrille
PUBLISHING

THE GREAT BRITISH
Sewing Bee

TESSA EVELEGH
foreword and practical tips by:
PATRICK GRANT & MAY MARTIN

Photography by Laura Edwards

Michelle

Tilly

Ann

Mark

Lauren

Jane

THE GREAT BRITISH SEWING

Stuart

Sandra

CONTENTS

78 Tunic

84 Pyjama trousers

112 Summer dress

120 Laundry bag

150 Tie cushion

154 Cook's apron

184 Camisole

190 Boyfriend shirt

220 Tote bag

228 Blouse with collar

FOREWORDS

Judging *The Great British Sewing Bee* was a really special time. My fellow judge Patrick Grant and I were keen to devise challenges that allowed contestants to really showcase both their technical skills and their own creativity. We, as judges, were looking for the perfect finish, which is an achievement at the best of times. Although the timeframe for each programme was tight, all the challenges set were manageable. Despite all the stress and competitiveness, the contestants got on incredibly well, bonding through the sewing tasks and supporting each other through all the ups and downs of the challenges.

Having taught dressmaking to both adults and children for many years, I've seen the 'typical' student change over the years from retired ladies taking up a new hobby to a new generation of young mums, hungry for knowledge because they didn't learn to sew at school. They're now getting together for their own sewing bees, taking photographs in my class so they can share skills with their friends, or blog them for an even wider audience. It's wonderful to see this growing desire to rediscover sewing, and we're all hoping that this series will enthuse a whole new wave of sewers.

May Martin

The Great British Sewing Bee set itself the task of finding Britain's best amateur sewer. Over its course we tested the sewers ability to sew and tailor everything from jackets to children's clothing, shirts to evening gowns, we tested their ability to cut patterns, to sew, to fit and to alter, all done under the glare of the lights, in front of the cameras and the watchful eyes of myself and my fellow judge, the astonishingly knowledgeable May Martin. I feel enormously privileged to work within the community of tailors on Savile Row and in judging this competition I was looking for the same level of commitment and natural ability with fabric from the contestants that I see every day in my workshop. As a nation we are collectively re-discovering the joy that comes in making clothes for ourselves, for our children, even simply altering or repairing something we have previously enjoyed wearing to give it renewed life.

Sewing is a straightforward and fine craft, engaging mentally, and in the case of hand-sewing rhythmic, almost hypnotic. It is also a forgiving craft, if you make a mistake you can simply unpick and start again. And it is something that men and women of any age can enjoy. Our sewers not only tackled the challenges set with great commitment and skill, they showed such enormous generosity and camaraderie with one another, and have also shown such a passion for the art of sewing and tailoring that I cannot help but feel that they will be an enormous inspiration to anyone who watches them. I know that they inspired May and myself.

Patrick Grant

THE JOY OF SEWING

The Great British Sewing Bee, presented by Claudia Winkleman, was the first national talent search for sewers of its kind. Whether you want to learn to stitch from scratch, dress yourself or dress your home, you'll find all you need to get yourself started in this book, which has been written to accompany the BBC2 TV series. Inspired by The Queen Mother's wartime sewing bees where women all over the country got together to make and mend uniforms for the war effort, the series sets out to find Britain's best non-professional sewers. One of the upshots of the programme, was that, despite the competitive element, as the series progressed, the contestants became really bonded with each other, united by their love of sewing in much the same way as the women who got together for the wartime sewing bees. The sewing and craft cafés are seeing much the same spirit where people can get together to learn an ancient skill and beginners and experienced alike can swap skills, tips and techniques.

Like any craft, it takes time to build sewing skills. Just like learning to drive, while the basics don't take long to master, you do need practice time to become really proficient. This doesn't mean you can't produce something lovely right from the start... and that is what this book is all about. It takes you step by step through all the basics skills, gives essential information on how to decipher paper patterns, lists the equipment needed, and teaches how to choose fabrics like a professional. But the main element of the book is a menu of fabulous projects – both fashion and furnishing – designed with the beginner in mind. You can easily obtain all the full-sized patterns for the projects by photocopying or scaling up the pattern pieces printed in the book, or by downloading 20 of the patterns in a format that can be easily printed on a home printer and then stuck together tile-style ready for use.

Woven through the book are fascinating historical cameos about the people who have influenced and loved sewing, patterns and fashions over the years, setting a perspective our very own twenty-first-century sewing cafés and *The Great British Sewing Bee*.

The Queen Mother's Sewing Bees

The wartime 'Stitch for Victory' sewing bees that inspired the TV series,
The Great British Sewing Bee.

Although Sewing Bees date back to colonial America, the most memorable must have been when the Queen Mother threw open the doors to Buckingham Palace's Blue Room, and invited women from every walk of life to join her sewing bees. The year was 1939 and the aim was to make clothes for the troops fighting in World War II.

The Queen was patron of the Women's Voluntary Service and wanted to encourage women at home to 'do their bit' for the war effort. Twice a week, she invited female members of the Household to stitch for victory. Together they would mend uniforms, make camouflage nets, blackout curtains, balaclavas and sweaters, exchanging stories as they sewed, on what were noisy, productive afternoons. With her strong Christian faith, Elizabeth held that 'life-is-for-living-and-working-at', and that included everyone, even the Queen of England. So Elizabeth metaphorically rolled up her sleeves and got on with it. With her warm, ready smile, she connected with people as a wartime morale booster. Her example inspired even high society women. Socialite beauty, Lady Diana Cooper literally 'mucked in', and was pictured in *Vogue* feeding pigs. The Queen's aim was to promote unity among women in the war effort, making everyone feel valued. Under her patronage, the Women's Voluntary Service set up highly productive sewing bees throughout the country, and in working together, the women found support through the dark days of wartime.

As the war progressed and fabric was harder to come by, clothes were rationed so women became more resourceful in making them last. The government issued leaflets on how to 'Make-do-and-mend', either transforming garments or extending their life. Women were resourceful, making shirts out of sheets, re-making children's out-grown clothes for younger ones, using parachute silk (a war-effort fabric that wasn't rationed) to make evening gowns. As the war progressed, women got together in sewing bees to share knowledge, skills and newly discovered ways to keep their families adequately dressed.

These wartime sewing bees had parallels with their Colonial American sewing bee forebears. In the eighteenth and nineteenth centuries, there were 'bees' of all kinds – logging bees, spinning bees, quilt-making bees and, of course, sewing bees. Everyone got together to make light work of arduous, drawn out or boring jobs, to get them done quickly (in the day), and to have fun whilst they were doing so. Many of the sewing bees were, in fact, quilt-making bees. Young girls made quilts for their dowries, often from worn-out shirts cut into little pieces and patched together in blocks to make the quilt top. Sometimes, the whole village would get together to make the quilts under the direction of one person. Children would be paid to thread needles, saving sewers stitching time, and at the end of the day, there'd be dancing to fiddlers' jigs, food and fun all round.

Most of us think these events are called bees because everyone works together as busy bees, just like the insects. Less evocatively, the word bee probably comes from Old English, ben or bene, which means 'boon', or being given extra help by neighbours. In any event, they are social events to carry out a communal task, and as the Queen Mother's Sewing Bees demonstrated, many hands really did make light work.

Ladies who worked in Buckingham Palace were invited by Queen Elizabeth (later the Queen Mother) to stitch for victory in the grand setting of the Blue Room. By setting up this sewing bee, the Queen encouraged women all over the country to get together in sewing bees for the war effort.

STARTING TO SEW

STOCKING THE SEWING BOX

A well-stocked sewing box is essential, whether you are sewing by hand or by machine. You don't need complicated tools or equipment and most of what you need to start sewing may already be familiar.

Needles

Using the right needles for the job will make your work infinitely easier and quicker. Needles should be kept in a needlebook as they can easily blunt when left to rattle around in a box or tin.

SHARPS are all-purpose needles with easy-to-thread eyes. Available in twelve sizes, the most useful are sizes 6 to 9.
BETWEENS are the short, fine needles with small eyes used by quilters to quickly work tiny, even stitches. These come in 12 sizes, but as quilting requires a fine needle, sizes 8 to 12 are most useful.
CREWEL or embroidery needles are long and have oval eyes to make quick work of threading stranded embroidery thread. The larger sizes 3 to 6 are the most useful as they are easiest to thread.
TAPESTRY and cross stitch needles are for use on canvas, aida and evenweave fabric. They have blunt ends so they can pass between the fabric threads without piercing them.
DARNING needles are long, sturdy, large eyed and blunt ended. This combination makes it easy to thread them with wool and to easily weave in and out of wool strands.
BEADING needles are long and very fine, so they can easily slip through the hole in the bead.
UPHOLSTERY demands its own particular needles, which are strong and sturdy. They include some that are very long for buttoning work and curved ones to slipstitch three-dimensional cushions.
MACHINE needles come in four point styles: sharps for general sewing, light ball for fine jerseys, medium ball for heavier-weight jerseys, and cutting point for PVC and leather. They range in sizes from No 60 (0.6mm) for silks to No 120 (1.2mm) for canvas. No 80 (0.8mm) is the size for medium-weight fabrics. The imperial equivalents are sizes 8 to 20. Always use the correct point style and size, otherwise the needle may break and damage the machine.

Thimble

Available in metal, plastic or silicon, a thimble protects the end of the finger used to push the needle through when hand sewing.

Needle threader

A fine wire loop that can be pushed through the eye of a needle for easy threading.

Pins

As with needles, choosing the right pins for the job will speed up the project. Keeping them in a pincushion will help to keep them sharp.

HOUSEHOLD pins are robust general-purpose pins.
DRESSMAKER'S pins are finer so they don't mark fabric.
BRIDAL or lace pins are the finest of all.
GLASS- or pearl-headed pins are longer than general household pins. Easier on the fingertips and easier to see (and therefore also easier remove when you need to).
QUILTER'S pins are extra-long glass-headed pins.

Bodkins

A professional tool used for threading through casings. There are two types: the first is a large blunt needle with a large eye for elastic; the second is a 'pinch' type and clasps ribbon ready to thread through a casing.

Safety pins

Among others things, safety pins can be used as improvised bodkins to thread elastic through casings.

Measuring tools

Just like carpenters, dressmakers are best advised to measure twice (at least) and cut once. The more accurately the pieces are measured, the more accurately they're likely to be cut and the better end result.

TAILOR'S MEASURING TAPE
This soft cloth tape is coated (usually with plastic) to prevent it stretching. Perfect for taking measurements during dressmaking, including body measurements.

STEEL TAPE
You'll need this for curtain making – both to measure up windows and the lengths of fabric during construction.

STEEL RULE
Choose a stable ruler made of steel or plastic that is at least 30 to 45cm (12 to 18in) long. This is handy for accurate measurements, and drawing straight lines. Professionals would also have a yardstick (metrestick).

SEWING GAUGE
This is a handy ruler about 15cm (6in) long that incorporates a slider/marker for accurate measurement of hems and small pieces such as collars and cuffs. It also incorporates a point to help with turning through collars.

Marking tools

Once you've cut out the fabric, you'll need to accurately transfer the markings from the paper or tissue pattern to all the layers of material. You'll also sometimes need to mark adjustments to garments during the making process. There are several ways to do this ranging from traditional tailor's chalk and tailor's tacks to specialist water-soluble and heat transfer pencils.

TAILOR'S CHALK
A fine chalk that readily marks fabric yet easily brushes off. Available in several colours, it comes in traditional squares or rounded triangular shapes, or in a self-sharpening container. This is more useful for making adjustments as it would be difficult to accurately transfer markings from the paper pattern pieces using chalk.

WATER-SOLUBLE DRESSMAKER'S PENCILS

These pencils are used for marking fabric, but can then be removed by water. Push the tip of the pencil through the pattern piece. Work on one layer of fabric, replace the pattern on the next layer and repeat the process.

HEAT TRANSFER PENCILS

Transfer markings easily by tracing them onto paper with these pencils, then ironing them onto the fabric.

DRESSMAKER'S CARBON AND TRACING WHEEL

A piece of carbon is placed between the pattern piece and every layer of fabric. The tracing wheel transfers the marks from the pattern onto all layers.

Cutting tools

Clean, accurate cuts are essential for the speed and success of any sewing project. When it comes to cutting tools, it is worth investing in the best. Quality scissors not only have sharp blades that have been properly ground, but they have been ergonomically designed. This means the tool is comfortable in the hand and the weight is appropriate for the job.

DRESSMAKER'S SHEARS

These shears must be very sharp, with blades at least 20cm (8in) long and handles that bend upwards so the fabric stays flat on the cutting surface. The best quality shears are heavy in the hand – this helps to steady them as you cut. Try them out. Most of your hand should fit in the lower handle and your thumb should feel comfortable in the top one. Save your dressmaker's shears just for fabrics – other materials can blunt them.

SPRING-LOADED SHEARS

These are not as heavy as traditional shears and have a spring that opens the blades so all you have to do is squeeze to cut. Possibly easier to handle if you have arthritis, but try them first. Not as long lasting as traditional shears as the spring can lose its effectiveness.

HOUSEHOLD SCISSORS

Use these to cut out the paper patterns to save blunting your fabric shears.

PINKING SHEARS

The zigzag blades of these cut a decorative edge whilst reducing the fraying (ravelling) of the fabric. This is one of the quickest and easiest ways to finish seams. Pinking shears can also be used to cut a decorative edge on fabrics, such as felt, that don't fray.

EMBROIDERY SCISSORS

Small and lightweight, use these to accurately snip threads and embroidery silks.

THREAD CLIPS

This spring-loaded tool fits neatly in your hand with a thumb-hole on the top. Small, lightweight and comfortable to use, it's great for quickly and neatly snipping away stray threads and embroidery silks.

ROTARY CUTTER

Looking much like a pizza cutter, rotary cutters are used mainly by quilters, to cut several layers of fabric at once. They need to be used in conjunction with a quilter's ruler on a cutting mat, both of which are marked out with lines and angles to help quilters cut accurate squares and triangles.

STITCH RIPPER

A small fork-like tool that makes quick work of undoing any mistakes.

Try this...

If you can't find a sewing box you like, check out a **DIY** store. Toolboxes with plenty of compartments can be ideal for storing your sewing needs. Plastic toolboxes are the best choice as they are lighter weight and therefore easier to carry.

TOOLS OF THE TRADE

As with any job, you need the right tools. Without them, your sewing will take longer, be more difficult and the finish will not be as professional. Thankfully, it's not overly expensive to set yourself up with a basic sewing kit. Here's what you need.

The sewing machine

The sewing machine is the biggest investment. It is also the most essential, so, if you're a complete beginner, before rushing out and buying one, you might prefer to start off by borrowing a machine, or trying a workshop that provides them. Having said that, basic home sewing machines are reasonably priced and bearing in mind the jobs they will be able to take on over the years, they are well worth the investment. Give yourself time when choosing. Go to a specialist who is prepared to give you a test run before buying. Think carefully about what you really need. It is easy to be persuaded by an expensive all-singing all-dancing computerised machine that offers fancy programmed embroidery when most of the time, you'll be using the straight stitch, zigzag, a decent buttonholer and possibly a few standard 'fancy' stitches.

Machine accessories

The simplest modern machine comes with a basic toolkit, including:

STANDARD ATTACHMENTS

An all-purpose foot for general sewing, a zip foot and a blind hem foot. There are often two spool caps of different sizes to hold the reel of thread in position on the top of the machine as you sew. You'll also get spare bobbins, needles and a stitch ripper. For sewing machine maintenance, you'll get a screwdriver and cleaning tool.

SPECIAL ATTACHMENTS

Most people find the basic toolkit enough for most jobs, though an invisible zip foot would be a useful extra buy. As you become more experienced, you may want to invest in a binder for neatly applying bias binding, rufflers, tuckers, and endless others. When buying, doublecheck that they are the correct ones for your machine – each manufacturer's are slightly different.

The overlocker

This is an expensive separate professional machine used to trim and finish off the edges of the seams in a single action. Because they cut the fabrics as it sews, you need to be a confident machinist before attempting to use overlockers as they have been known to cut into the main garment. An overlocker is not essential; there are many alternative ways to finish seam edges (see pages 54–55). However, most proficient sewers love the finish their overlockers bring to their work.

USING YOUR MACHINE

Whatever machine you have, there will be times when it just doesn't seem to behave. Just like with a car or computer, you'll become increasingly proficient with your sewing machine as you use it. As each model is different, get to know your own by studying the manual. Here are some tips to get you going and troubleshooting hints for when you get exasperated.

Before you start

Start by selecting the right stitch length for the fabric. Generally you'll need shorter stitches for fine fabrics and longer ones if you're stitching heavier fabrics. Cut two squares of fabric to represent a seam of the garment you plan to make. Now work a line of stitches on the bias. The stitches should look even with no loops on the front or the back of the fabric. Pull the fabric to check the stitches don't break. Now look closer at the stitches. The top thread and bottom (bobbin) thread should lock together where the fabric thicknesses meet. If the bobbin thread is being pulled to the top surface or the top thread down to the under layer, the tension may need adjusting. However, a lot of 'tension' problems can actually be traced to threading basics. So first, try these steps.

WIND THE BOBBIN

Wind a bobbin from the reel of thread you are using for the project – then the top and bottom thread work in harmony and will not fight each other.

REMOVE ANY STRAY THREADS

Clear out any threads under the throat plate or between the tension disks.

CHECK THE BOBBIN

Is the thread running freely? If not, remove the bobbin from its housing and unreel any jammed thread. Re-wind the bobbin, take off any remaining thread, then re-wind it slowly following the manufacturer's instructions to ensure it's evenly wound.

CHECK THE NEEDLE

Ensure you're using the correct needle. Silks and chiffons require finer needles. Change the needle if necessary.

RE-THREAD THE MACHINE

Start by making sure the spool cap that holds the thread in position is the right size for the reel. Now re-thread, ensuring the thread passes freely through all the thread guides and the presser foot is down before threading the needle. Re-try the stitch sample. If there's still a problem, you'll need to make a small adjustment to the tension.

ADJUST THE TENSION

Machines are tension-corrected before being sold, so the tension dial is most likely to be set at 4. If you generally sew on a tension other than 4, take the machine back to the supplier to re-set the tension. The only adjustment to the tension you may need to make will probably be to allow for an especially fine or particularly heavy fabric. If your machine is currently set at 4 and, after all the above checks, your top stitches still look loopy, turn the dial to a higher number; if the underside stitches look loopy, you'll need to turn the dial to a lower number. If you're using a more regular fabric for your next project, you should expect to readjust the tension dial back to 4.

Troubleshooting

NEEDLE JAMS

Check the needle hasn't worked loose in the shaft. Re-fit it and ensure the screw is properly tightened. Check you're using the right foot – if you switch to zigzag stitch, change the foot to one that allows for a swing needle.

NEEDLE BREAKS

It might have hit metal – a pin or zip teeth. It might also have worked loose in the shaft and broken because it hit the throat plate. Replace the needle.

STITCHES WON'T FORM

Check there is thread on the bobbin and that the machine is properly threaded.

BOTTOM THREAD BREAKS

Remove the bobbin, clean out any threads from the bobbin housing. Re-wind the bobbin and re-thread the machine.

TOP THREAD BREAKS

Check you're using the right needle for the fabric. If not, replace the needle, then re-thread the machine.

UNDERSTANDING PAPER PATTERNS

Commercial patterns are the sewing equivalent of cookery recipes. The envelope and its contents give you all the information needed to make the garment. It's a blueprint, if you like, because no two handmade garments will ever be identical. You can add your own flair with the choice of fabrics, trimmings and buttons, and even adapt the pattern a little if you like. The symbols and diagrams might look intimidating, but once you start using them, you'll find them as easy to follow as any recipe.

Start at the back

Once you've chosen the design you like, decipher the back of the pattern packet. You'll find technical sketches of the back views, showing the positions of any seams, fastenings and trimmings. The rest of the back of the envelope is given over to all the information you need to buy the materials. Here's what to expect:

🔑 *Body measurements for all the standard sizes included in the pattern, given in both metric (cm) and imperial (in).*

🔑 *Garment measurements showing the exact finished size of the clothing once made. This allows for ease and movement.*

🔑 *Fabric requirements for each size, including the amounts needed for different fabric widths. A suitable fabrics list gives fibre options.*

🔑 *Haberdashery (or notions) list of all you'll need to complete the garment: zips, buttons, elastic, etc.*

Next look inside

Inside the envelope, you'll find an instruction sheet and full-sized tissue pattern pieces. Most patterns are multi-sized so there may be a different cutting line (solid, dotted or dashed) to follow for each size. The pattern pieces may also be marked with symbols that relate to the instructions. Here are the most common symbols:

⟷ *Straight of grain – place this line parallel to the side edge of the fabric to ensure the piece is cut in line with the grain*

↧—↧ *Foldline – place this edge on the foldline of the fabric in order to cut a perfectly symmetrical piece*

═══ *Adjustment – lengthen or shorten a piece between these lines*

◇◆▽▼ *Notches – match separate fabric pieces by aligning the notches*

●●○○ *Dots – these indicate, for example, the beginning and end of gathers or easing stitches*

↤•••○ *Darts – theses indicate where contour shaping is to be added*

⊕ ✕ *Buttonhole – these indicated where a buttonhole is to be sewn*

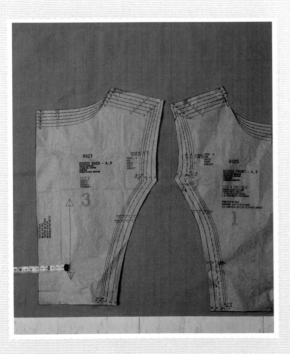

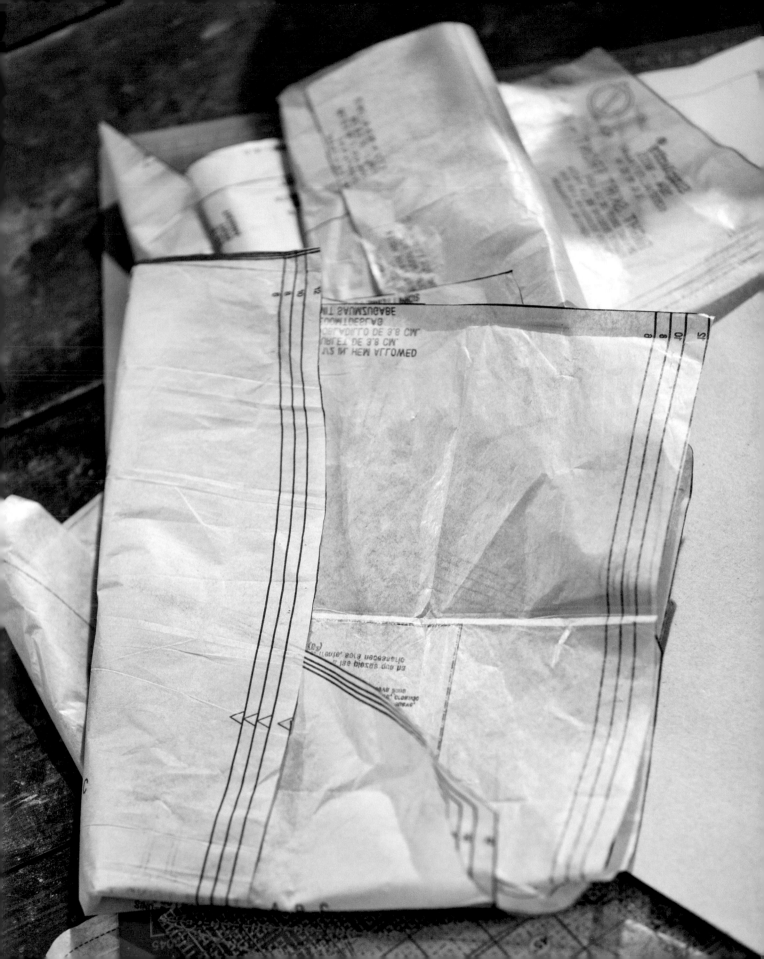

Prepare the pattern pieces

Most pattern packs contain several variations of one or more designs. Whichever version of a particular design you choose to make, you will need only some of the numbered tissue pattern pieces. There will be a list of which pieces are needed for each option, so start by carefully cutting them out along the cutting line given for your size using paper or household scissors. Finally, iron each tissue pattern piece using a cool iron to remove any folds or creases.

Prepare the fabric

Before you begin to sew, ensure your fabric has been pre-shrunk, otherwise the final made-up garment may become distorted the first time you launder it. When you buy your fabric, check the care label on the roll or bolt. If it's a dry clean material then the fabric should remain stable so there is no need to launder it. If not, wash, dry and iron the fabric.

Next, make sure the fabric is lying straight across the cross grain – the horizontal threads of the fabric should run at right angles to the woven side edge, or selvedge. The best way to do this is to pull out a single thread across the width of the fabric to give a straight line to cut along. You won't be able to do this with jacquards because of the way they are woven. For these, you'll need to draw a straight line across the grain. Do this by lining up a gridded quilter's ruler or set-square against the selvedge so you can draw a line at right angles to it across the width of the fabric. Cut along the marked line to ensure the fabric edge is perfectly straight.

It is essential the threads of the fabric are straight and the pattern pieces are cut on the correct grain, with the straight of grain arrows parallel to the direction of the woven threads, otherwise the fabric – and consquently the finished garment – may not hang correctly.

Take the measurements

Whilst couturiers and theatre costumiers make each garment to fit a specific client or actor, ready-to-wear fashion comes in off-the-peg sizes... but few of us are off-the-peg people. If we're lucky, we might have the requisite off-the-peg bust, waist and hip measurement, but we might also have a longer back, wider shoulders and longer or shorter arms or legs. Making your own garments has the huge advantage of allowing for pattern adjustments before we even begin to cut out the fabric.

Professional tailors take endless measurements and make infinite adjustments, but for the home dressmaker, even a few measurements can make all the difference to a garment's fit and fall. The most useful measurements to take are:

- *Full bust* – around the bust at its fullest point
- *Bust point* – from the shoulder down to the fullest point of the bust
- *Waist* – around the narrowest part of the waist
- *Back waist* – from the vertebra at the base of the neck to the small of the back
- *Hip* – around the hips at the widest part of the abdomen and buttocks
- *Sleeve length* – from the shoulder to the wrist via the bent elbow
- *Side length* – from the waist to the desired length of the skirt, shorts or trousers

Adjust the pattern

There are two parallel lines at points of the pattern where they can be adjusted whilst retaining the basic shape of the piece. If you need to shorten the piece, make a fold between the lines to shorten it by the required amount. If you want to lengthen it, cut between the lines, then use masking tape and a strip of spare paper to elongate the pattern piece.

If you want to make widthways adjustments, remember that because each pattern piece represents a quarter of your body, you will need to enlarge or reduce it by a quarter of the overall difference between the body measurement (NOT garment measurement) stated on the pattern and your own body measurement. So, if your waist is 2.5cm (1in) smaller than the body measurement stated on the pattern, you will want to reduce each piece by 6mm (¼in). If it is a small amount (which it should be if you have a multi-sized pattern), it's probably easiest to take this amount off each side seam.

Mr Beeton and the dressmaking pattern

The cook's husband who put the first dressmaking patterns into women's magazines.

Most of us have heard of Mrs Beeton and her eponymous cookbook, but it was her publisher husband, Samuel Beeton, who published *The Englishwoman's Domestic Magazine*, which was to change the face of women's magazines forever. And the difference was largely down to the dressmaking patterns that Mr Beeton decided to give away with the magazine from 1863. In the early nineteenth century, neither dressmaking patterns nor popular women's magazines existed. The magazines that were published, were extravagant affairs featuring the latest Parisian styles for wealthy women of leisure to have copied by their couture dressmakers. Most 'ordinary' women had to rely on a visit to the local dressmaker for stock styles, or show them a picture and hope for the best. But Samuel Beeton recognised the rise of the middle class housewife who wanted to dress in the latest styles whilst keeping up standards at home as befit her upwardly mobile husband. Seeing a new enthusiasm for dressmaking, Samuel Beeton included one-sized traceable patterns in every issue of *The Englishwoman's Domestic Magazine*. The patterns were in their infancy and not nearly as sophisticated as their modern-day equivalents as readers had to trace them off and adjust them to their own size... though the astute Mr Beeton generally published simple shapes, such as underwear, loose jackets and blouses, with a less demanding fit. However, enthusiasm for home dressmaking was established, and by the time fashion shapes became more simplified in the 1920s and 1930s, cheap mass market tissue patterns had not only become widely available in their own right, but good end results were more achievable. In those days, though, tissue patterns were often hole-punched, rather than printed. It wasn't until after World War II that printed patterns with multi-sized cutting lines and markings became generally available, making professional-looking home-sewing so much more achievable! By the 1960s a new, younger generation was inspired to make their own, encouraged by the simple lines of current designers such as Mary Quant.

All through these decades, and right up to the 1990s, many women's magazines, continued to print patterns either on their pages, or as special send-for offers in true Samuel Beeton tradition. And while all those lines, dashes, dots and triangles may look confusing to first-time pattern users, they are actually, brilliant blueprints that enable even novice sewers to produce professional-looking results.

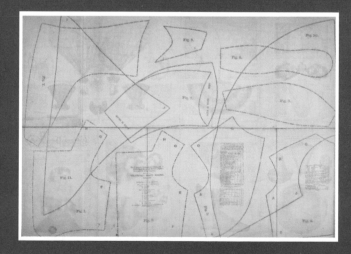

Try this...

If you're making a skirt, dress or corset with several panels that look very similar, make sure you match the seams correctly by thread-marking them with different colours. For example, when you come to pin the seams, you know to match the red threads on one piece with the red threads on the next one, blue with blue, green with green, and so on.

Lay out the pattern pieces

The instruction sheet inside the pattern envelope will include a layout plan for each garment option, which shows you how to cut out all the necessary pattern pieces from your length of fabric. This cutting guide will be marked with any relevant symbols, such as the straight of grain and foldline for any pieces that must be cut from folded fabric. If you decide to work out your own layout, make sure that you always follow these two markings on the pattern.

NAP AND DIRECTIONAL PATTERNS

If you are using a fabric with a nap (a pile or a weave such as herringbone that runs in one direction), or one with a pattern that goes in one direction, a tartan, for example, or a repeated motif, make sure all the pieces run in the same direction. This may require extra fabric.

CENTRING PATTERNS

A fabric with a large motif pattern repeat will need to be centred on the garment. Sometimes, it is easier to do this on a single layer of fabric so you can make sure each piece is centred accurately. If you do fold the fabric, make sure the fold runs accurately down the centre of the motif, or between two motifs.

PINNING

Place the pieces in position on the fabric. Pin any in position on the fold, smoothing the pattern out as you do so. Next, pin along the straight of grain of the other pieces. Measure from the grain line out to the selvedge (the finished edges running down either side of the fabric) in several places to ensure the pattern piece is lying straight. Pin it in position along the grain line. Now use your hand to smooth out from this line out towards the edges of the pattern piece to make sure it is lying flat, then pin in position.

Cut out the fabric pieces

Use dressmaker's shears to cut out the pattern pieces from your fabric, using long clean cuts for a smart finish. Cut out any notches as you come to them.

Make your marks

Once all the fabric pieces are cut out, you need to transfer the markings such as darts, buttons, buttonholes, tuck positions and dots that mark the positioning of pockets, gathering and easing, for example. Everything needs to be marked on all the layers of fabric. There are several ways to do this.

USING A TRACING WHEEL AND DRESSMAKER'S CARBON

This is the quickest and easiest method. First, check the carbon (which comes in packs of several colours) on a spare piece of fabric. Choose a colour that shows up on your fabric, whilst being its closest match. Once you're ready to go, place a piece of carbon between the tissue paper pattern piece and each layer of fabric so the transferable side of the carbon marks the wrong side of the fabric. Use double-sided carbon where there are two layers of fabric. Simply run the tracer wheel over the lines you want to mark. Where there's a dot, trace a small cross.

USING MARKER PENS AND PENCILS

These can only mark one layer at a time. Marking the wrong side of the fabric, push the pen or pencil through the tissue to the fabric at points you want to mark. Reposition the tissue on the second layer of fabric and repeat. Draw in lines, such as dart lines using the marker and ruler.

USING THREAD MARKING

Also called tailor's tacks, the only equipment you need for this is a needle and contrast thread. Here's how to do it.

✎ *Thread up the needle with double thread but do not knot the end.*

✎ *Make long very loopy stitches along any lines you want to mark and cut the thread long at the end of the line. For dots, take one small stitch but leave both ends of the threads long.*

✎ *Now snip the loops made by the stitches. You should have a line of long, cut double threads marking, for example, the line of a dart.*

✎ *Remove the tissue pattern. Now lift the top layer of fabric a little and snip the threads between the layers of fabric. Both layers will be left with little tufts of marker threads.*

Part of the thrill and inspiration for sewing-your-own is the treasure trove of fabrics that come in an infinite combination of colours, textures and patterns. From pretty printed cottons to textured wool tweeds, delicate laces to rich brocades and damasks, there's endless potential for creating something special that expresses your own individual sense of style and flair. Choosing the fabric and trimmings is one of the most important steps in the design process.

Furnishing fabrics

Most of these are more heavy-weight than fashion fabrics, as they need to provide plenty of drape for curtains and, more importantly, be able to withstand the constant wear and tear demanded of upholstery. You'll also find sheers in the furnishing fabric department, designed to let light into the room while protecting privacy. They can be made from loose-woven cotton organdie, linen or fine synthetics. At 150cm (60in) wide or more, furnishing fabrics are wider than fashion fabrics, designed to deal with larger-scale projects.

Fashion fabrics

You'll find these grouped in various different sections within the store – not just by fibre type, but also by pattern. So there may be a cottons section, which is sub-divided into plains, printed patterns and wovens. Most fashion fabrics are 115cm (45in) wide, though some are 150cm (60in) wide. This makes a big difference to the amount of fabric you need to buy and most patterns list the quantities required for each width.

Additional fabrics

As well as the main fabrics, there is a wide choice of 'supporting' materials, which are used to create extra body and give a more luxurious finish to both garments and curtains.

LINING FABRICS

These come in a rainbow of colours, made from silk-like acetate for garments and cotton sateen for curtains. You can, of course, use any other fabric for lining, though they should generally be lighter weight than the main fabric, supporting rather than changing the shape and drape of the item.

INTERLININGS

Used to add extra support and structure, interlinings are available in a variety of weights. Traditionally, they were stitched into position, although now many can be ironed on.

WADDING

Wadding (or batting) for quiltmaking, padded jackets and upholstery is available in many weights, from 70 to 475 grams (2 to 14oz) per square metre.

Woven wool patterns

Fabrics are made up of three elements: the fibre, the way in which it is woven and how the pattern is achieved. These three fabrics are all twill-woven wool and the pattern is built up within the weave by threading up the loom with different colours in a particular order, the geometric patterns (including the classic dogtooth at the bottom) are created during the weaving process (see opposite page).

MAKING THE RIGHT CHOICE

It's the colour and pattern of a fabric that we're initially attracted to, but there are many more considerations before you're ready to make your choice. Is it fit for purpose? How does it drape? If you have already chosen a dressmaking pattern, check the back of the envelope and choose from the suggested list. Home furnishing projects are a little less complicated. If you're making curtains or scatter cushions, any furnishing fabric should work. But for anything that you may sit on, you will need to choose only from labelled upholstery fabric that will be able to stand the wear and tear. Whether you're working on a fashion or soft-furnishing project, run through this checklist to make sure that your choice will work with the design and is of good quality.

UNROLL A LENGTH of the fabric and check the size of the pattern repeat against your chosen design. Large patterns, for example, won't be suitable for dresses made up of several small pieces. Stripes, plaids, one-way patterns and the way the pile lies on a fabric such as velvet (which is known as nap), can affect the suitability and quantity needed for the design; check the fabric notes on the back of the pattern envelope.

HOLD THE FABRIC up to the light to assess the density of the weave. The looser the weave, the more easily it will fray and you will need to spend extra care when finishing the seams.

CHECK THE QUALITY as generally (but not always), the denser the weave, the better the quality. Some loose-weave sheer fabrics, such as cotton organdie, have been constructed and treated in a particular way to give them a crisp finish with excellent drape that is permanent, even through washing. But beware of choosing a pretty pattern on a loose weave that appears to have more body than you would expect. Many fabrics are treated, or 'dressed' for extra body, but this soon washes out.

So how can you gauge quality? Here are clues to help. Feel the weight: is it appropriate for the type of fabric? Cast your eye over a length of the fabric to check for colour inconsistencies or flaws within the weave. Look at the printed pattern (if there is one): is it parallel with the edges? Do stripes run straight or are they running slightly off the straight of grain?

TRY OUT THE DRAPE to asses if the fabric is soft and flowing or whether it has plenty of body? Hold the fabric in the way it will drape when made up. For example, if it's going to be gathered, gather some up in your hand to see how it falls.

STRETCH IT with the grain and across the bias to check how much it gives and whether or not that works with your chosen design.

ASSESS ITS WEARABILITY and laundry requirements by checking the care label. Every roll of fabric should have a care label and a fibre content list. Crush the fabric in your hand to see how it creases and how readily it springs back.

Hard workers

The honest weaves and unpretentious designs of traditional heavy-duty cotton utility fabrics have become very popular in recent years – but this time as furnishing fabrics. The top fabric is a ticking, traditionally twill-woven with dark blue or charcoal stripes and used to make pillows. Naturally robust enough even for upholstery, it has been resurrected as a smart furnishing fabric in a wide range of colours and stripe variations. The lower two fabrics are variations on traditional plain-weave floursack materials (see opposite page).

Natural fibres

Before scientific advances saw the invention of synthetic fibres, all fabrics were made from natural fibres. These are generally still seen as more desirable than synthetic: they all have a subtle natural sheen and are more comfortable against the skin. Most (although not all) are easier to sew as they are inclined to be less slippery. Since the introduction of the first man-made fibres at the beginning of the twentieth century, synthetics have become ever more sophisticated. Increasingly, fibres are mixed to combine the advantages of their different qualities. For example, more and more ready-to-wear garments made using mainly natural fibre fabrics also include a small percentage of spandex (Lycra) as it helps the garment to keep its shape. As a sewer, it is useful to understand each fibre's particular qualities so you can properly assess the fabric you are buying.

COTTON

The most widely used natural fibre, cotton is highly versatile, so it can be woven into endless different weights and qualities and dyed in myriad shades. It is also very resilient, and so can be given special finishes to improve the body and wear. Easy to launder and cool on the skin, it is a favourite breathable fabric for summer and makes for excellent winter layering under warmer outer layers.

Sewing user friendliness: very

WOOL

Sheep provide most of our wool, but it can also be spun from goats' coats (cashmere and mohair), rabbit (angora) or llama (alpaca, vicuna). Unlike fur or hair, wool has a naturally crimped quality that makes it easy to weave into many different weights and qualities, from fine challis, which is made to use for dresses, to elegant worsteds for suits and coarser tweeds. Wool does not crease easily and is valued by tailors because it can be steamed, sculpted and encouraged into shape. It dyes well into beautiful subtle colours. Designed to protect animals in cold climates, wool naturally keeps you warm in winter. However, it is a high-maintenance fabric, holds water, shrinks readily and pills easily, so is best dry cleaned. For sewers, it is not slippery, but can fray easily.

Sewing user friendliness: easy

LINEN

Spun from the long, waxy fibres of the flax plant, linen has a natural lustre and three times the strength of cotton. It doesn't take dye as well as cotton, which results in richer, plain colours where the pattern is generally woven into rather than printed onto the fabric. Because it creases readily, people either love or avoid linen. On the plus side, linen presses beautifully, looks sophisticated, and linings and interlinings can help reduce creasing in the finished garment. Very cool on the skin, it is an excellent summer fabric.

Sewing user friendliness: very

Cotton variations

Here's a sample of different kinds of cotton weaves that can also be used in combination with other fibres. From top left, clockwise: Small-scale printed pin dots are a patchwork favourite; crinkled white stripes teamed with flat green are classic small-scale seersucker; cotton jersey is a knitted fabric that offers a soft stretch drape; printed cotton comes in endless colours and designs; woven stripes look the same on both sides of the fabric and naturally follow the straight of grain; gingham is a popular tightly woven cotton, best known for its checked designs in various sizes.

SILK

This fine, lustrous fibre is spun by silkworms as they make their cocoons. Silk is an excellent insulator that evolved to keep the pupae at an even temperature whatever the outside conditions. In turn, it will keep you cool in summer while providing surprising warmth when needed. Originating in China, silk can be woven into richly coloured fabrics from fine chiffons to rich exotic brocades. Silk is a soft, fluid fabric that skims the contours for lingerie and feels wonderful against the skin, but its naturally slippery quality makes it something of a challenge to sew.

Sewing user friendliness: tricky

Synthetic fibres

Man-made fabrics are becoming increasingly sophisticated and it's no longer true, for example, that natural fibres have the monopoly on breathability. With a view to improving fabrics for sportswear, the textiles industry has invested heavily in wickable fabrics that draw moisture away from the skin. Sportswear has also been the inspiration behind super-stretch fibres such as spandex (Lycra). This can be used as a pure 100 per cent fabric, or incorporated into fabrics that are made up mainly of natural fibres but could do with a little extra elasticity to pull them back into shape. Each synthetic has different qualities and the main ones are outlined in more detail in the Fabric Dictionary (pages 248–250). However, synthetics are generally shinier, more slippery and easier to care for than their natural cousins. Many also have a lot more stretch. For these reasons, they can be more difficult to handle than natural fabrics.

Sewing user friendliness: moderate

Judge the drape

Although you might expect a fine, loose woven silk like this to have little or no body, this is not always the case. Depending on how it has been treated and woven, even the finest fabric could have plenty of drape. Hold the material up on the diagonal, and if the folds fall full and wide like this, you can be sure it will have plenty of body, and even if you plan to use it only as a 'flat' panel, it will have more life and will look crisper at the window (see opposite page).

TRIMMINGS AND FASTENINGS

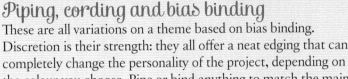

The secret to successful use of trimmings is to add them in a similar way to seasoning a recipe. Used sparingly, they add interest, intensify the ingredients and bring personality to the dish. As the trimmings are an essential part of the design, you need to choose and buy them at the same time as the main fabric. Here are some of the main types.

Piping, cording and bias binding

These are all variations on a theme based on bias binding. Discretion is their strength: they all offer a neat edging that can completely change the personality of the project, depending on the colour you choose. Pipe or bind anything to match the main fabric for elegant restrained style, or choose a vibrant contrast for a more extrovert look. Because piping, cording and bias binding are neat and discreet, they'll never overwhelm the piece, so you can afford to be brave with the colour if you so wish.

Bias binding is made from strips of fabric cut across the grain at 45 degrees to the straight edge. You can buy bias binding in a selection of widths and many colours, or you can make your own, and then use it to bind edges (see pages 70-71). Piping is bias binding that is stitched into, rather than over, the seam. Cording is piping with a cord running through it (confusingly, most of us know this as piping). You can buy the cord in a range of sizes from haberdashery shops and departments.

Ribbons and bows

Ribbons range from glossy double satin and sheer organza to exotic jacquard woven, chunky grosgrain and luxurious velvet in widths of 3mm (⅛in) to a bold 75mm (3in). They're generally designed to be surface stitched onto the piece, although wider ribbons can be stitched between seams for a piping effect. Use them in contrast to the main fabric to make a statement or more discreetly to add quality (down the inside of a button band of a cardigan, for example, so it is glimpsed when the garment is open).

Braids, fringes and tapes

Richly woven braids with their textured edges, are generally surface mounted on furnishings or heavier garments, such as jackets and coats. Fringes of all kinds – fabric, beaded, feathered – are usually mounted on braid, which is used as a base for stitching the fringe into the seam.

Twill and other woven tapes have their roots in utility pyjama tape. Often made in cotton, they are now available in a wide range of widths, colours and designs with a natural, unpretentious appeal.

Ribbon ranges

Ribbon trimmings can totally change the personality of a garment. These represent some of the main types, from bottom left: narrow green velvet is a pretty, feminine choice for eveningwear; red gingham, available in many widths and bright colours, lends a fun, country feel; the sheer cream organza adds pretty, feminine appeal; striped grosgrain was the ribbon of choice for Edwardian boaters (straw hats), and is still very popular today for both men's and women's garments; pure silk picot edged ribbon would add quality to any garment, especially in this restrained mossy green shade.

Keeping it together

You can either keep your fastenings secret, hidden from view so as not to spoil the line of the garment, or you can promote them, letting them multi-task as trimmings. This is not a new thing: buttons have always had trimming potential – not only in their intrinsic style, but also in how you use them. You might make a statement by fastening a coat using two huge buttons, or you may design a long row of tiny pearl buttons all the way down the back of a wedding dress. Both have a dramatic effect on the garment. Revealed zips can also be used as part of a design, immediately transforming what might have been a classic item to one with utility edginess. With the recent fashion for underwear as outerwear, rows of revealed hooks and eyes allude to corsetry while stud fasteners, especially larger ones, imply camping and outdoor life.

Buttons

There's something irresistible about buttons. They can be made from almost any material and be big, small, simple or intricate and have the power to completely change the look of a garment. When buying, try to

visualise the space the buttons will occupy to make sure there's an overall balance. For example, two large buttons might make a statement, but six might use the space better, providing a better balance.

Zips

One of the most useful fastenings available, there are several different kinds of zips, suitable for different situations ranging from tiny nylon ones for children's clothes to huge outdoor types suitable for luggage, camping equipment and marquees.

METAL zips are the original, consisting of two lines of interlocking teeth set within a tape. They're generally bulkier and showier than their nylon equivalents.
NYLON zips come in myriad colours with perfectly matched tapes and teeth; they are the most popular type.
INVISIBLE zips have a pair of coils instead of two rows of teeth. These sit neatly behind the tapes when closed and so the zip just looks like part of the seam.
OPEN ENDED zips are for garments, such as jackets.
CONTINUOUS zips made from nylon are also sold by the metre (yard) with one slider per metre. They're used where you need long lengths, such as for upholstery and window-seat cushion covers. Simply snip off the length needed using household scissors.

Hooks, snaps and secret fastenings

HOOKS AND EYES for their size, have extraordinary strength. Skirt and trouser hooks, for example, need to take the strain of a close fit and constant movement.
SNAPS that are sewn on are traditional, but you can also buy a wide range of the no-sew snaps, studs, rivets and jeans buttons. These are fixed in position using pliers or a special tool, which usually comes as part of the kit.
ELASTIC might not be a fastening but it does enable getting in and out of garments. Available from thread-like shirring elastic that can be used with a sewing machine to 75mm (3in) wide.
HOOK-AND-LOOP TAPE (Velcro) provides strong, discreet fastenings. It is available in strips that can be cut to length or dots.

Beau Brummell and the modern suit

The eighteenth-century dandy who is the father of modern masculine bespoke tailoring.

Change might be the lifeblood of women's fashions, but unbelievably, the basic design of men's suits has hardly changed for 200 years. Back in the late eighteenth century, French-inspired male fashion was all breeches and bows in silks and brocades, brightly coloured trimmings, wigs and even high heels! But in the 1790s, all that was set to change...

The change was largely down to George Bryan Brummell, nicknamed Beau, who cut a dash in sober colours and streamlined silhouettes, and is largely credited with getting men out of breeches and into trousers.

Charming and intelligent with a razor-sharp wit, although Beau was a 'mere' politician's son, he moved in aristocratic circles, counting the Prince Regent (the future George IV) a close friend and became something of a fashion oracle for him. Beau worked with his tailor, Jonathan Meyer, moving from what was essentially dressmaking to what is now known as bespoke tailoring. He briefed Meyer to create sleek cut-to-fit garments for a new, elegant look that everyone, including the Prince wanted to emulate.

Historically, Beau's new ideas came at exactly the right time, during what is known as the French Revolution's 'Reign of Terror' when the French King, Queen and numerous noble families were sent to the guillotine. English nobility were understandably keen to distance themselves from all things French, and especially the elaborate dress associated with the upper echelons of society. Beau's masculine, understated elegance answered a much-needed change of style. His tailor, Jonathan Meyer, would have been a man of outstanding skill; an expert cutter who could respond to the ideas of an original thinker. This is the heritage on which Savile Row, London's famous 'Mecca' of bespoke tailoring was built.

Sadly for Beau, there was no happy ending. His decadent lifestyle, running with the wealthy landed set was unsustainable on his small inheritance. Debt sent him into exile in France where he eventually died at the age of 62 in a French asylum, driven insane by syphilis. But Beau did leave an enduring legacy for menswear. Practical, unfussy and elegant, his ideas made fashionable clothes accessible for all men and even more than 200 years later he's still got most modern men wearing his trousers.

BASIC SEWING SKILLS

START SEWING

Sewing from scratch seems intimidating, but start with something simple and suddenly it all seems less daunting. The key is to choose a simple pattern that doesn't have too many fiddly bits like collars, inset sleeves and buttonholes. Each of our projects is designed for new (and newish) sewers, and some incorporate 'cheats' to make the skills even more beginner-friendly. Take the time to build up your skills as you set out on your sewing journey. If there's anything you don't understand, refer to Basic Skills Section which is a fully illustrated guide to elementary sewing knowhow.

Start with your work station

Have a flat, clear surface for cutting out. In the absence of a large cutting table, this could be the floor. When sewing, position the sewing machine on a clear table so the fabric can lie flat and move freely as you sew.

Keep your work neat

Snip off trailing threads and badly frayed edges as you go – if you don't, they'll soon get jammed under the needle and snarl up the machine.

Tacking knowhow

To begin with, pin and temporarily stitch (tack) at every stage so you can make sure all the pieces are lying correctly before you introduce the sewing machine. As you become more experienced, you'll sometimes be able to go straight from pinning to machining. This will depend on what you're trying to do and the fabric you're working with. The project instructions don't tell you to tack every time because that will depend on your experience level. But there are times when you really should tack, such as setting in a sleeve or putting in a zip, and at those times, the instructions include tacking.

Handling fabric

One of the most important sewing lessons to learn is how to 'ease' the fabric. When making garments, sometimes the cut pieces look as if they'll never fit together. Set-in sleeves are an example. The sleeve head is obviously larger than the armhole. By running easing stitches and pulling them up to fit the armhole, you're making the top of the sleeve curve over the shoulder. Sometimes, easing is more subtle and you need to pull one piece of fabric to fit the piece you're sewing it to. All this you will learn-by-doing and improve with experience.

Keep pressing

An ironing board and hot iron are key players in any sewing room. Experienced dressmakers can't stress enough how often you need to press your piece. This is because if all the seams are good and flat, the pieces will fit together better. Also, the steam in the iron helps to even out stitches and mould pieces into shape (such as round the curve of an armhole). The more steam you can use and the hotter the iron, the better. For safety, always test the heat on a spare piece of fabric. Not all fabrics can stand too much heat; the aim is to get the iron as hot as possible for that particular fabric.

✄ SEAMS

Generally seams need to be pressed open. Sometimes, both parts of the seam allowance need to be pressed in the same direction. The project instructions explain when this is needed.

✄ GATHERS

Gathers should be opened out, not flattened. Where gathers have been stitched into a band, lay the widest part of the fabric on the ironing board and hold up the gathered edge. Starting at the flat part of the fabric, iron in towards the gathers.

✄ CURVES

The aim is to retain the shape, not to flatten it. Put the curve over the end of the ironing board, choosing the pointed end or the squared end, depending on the size or shape of the curve. Alternatively, hold the piece up vertically and iron into the curve. Depending on the shape of the piece, you may have to 'roll' it as you iron.

✄ KEEP IT CLEAN

Use a cleaning stick to keep the sole plate of the iron clear of residue.

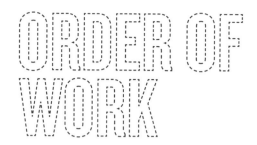
ORDER OF WORK

Working in a logical order is key to a professional finish. Here's a 'template' of good practice that can be adapted to suit individual projects.

1 LAUNDER THE FABRIC
Not all new fabrics are pre-shrunk, so launder your material following the care label before cutting out. Miss this step at your peril. You may put your heart and soul into making a garment, only to find it loses body, shrinks, or becomes misshapen the first time it's washed.

2 PRESS THE FABRIC
Press out any creases and folds using plenty of steam and the hottest iron setting possible that suits the fabric. Pull it back into shape if necessary. Trim any uneven edges.

3 PREPARE THE PAPER PATTERN PIECES
Cut out the pieces needed for the garment and iron them using a very cool iron. Adjust them if necessary.

4 CUT OUT THE FABRIC PATTERN PIECES
Follow the cutting layout provided for each of the garment projects. For most home furnishings, it's more a case of cutting squares and rectangles to size (see page 25).

5 TRANSFER THE MARKINGS
Ensure you transfer all the markings on the pattern pieces to all the fabric layers (see page 25).

6 STITCH THE DARTS
These are also easiest to handle whilst the piece is at its least complicated.

7 PUT IN THE ZIP
Put the zip in at as early a stage as possible as that way, there will be less fabric to handle and the pieces will still be flat. Depending on the design (for example, if a dress zip runs through separate bodice and skirt pieces), it might not be possible to make this the first step.

8 PIN, TACK, STITCH AND FINISH THE MAIN SEAMS
Beginners will want to go through all these steps at every stage. As you become more experienced, you may not want to tack every step. It is good to finish all the seams as you work (see pages 54–55). If you have an overlocker you may prefer to finish the seams before stitching them.

9 STITCH ON FACINGS
Once the facings are stitched on, the garment is much more stable and easier to handle. Also, all the raw edges under them are protected from fraying.

10 STITCH THE BODICE TO THE SKIRT OR STITCH ON THE WAISTBAND
This is one of the final stages as, after this point, the garment becomes larger and more difficult to handle.

11 PREPARE AND INSERT SLEEVES
If the garment has a dropped sleeve that doesn't need easing, a loose shirt, for example, it can be easier to put the sleeve in before sewing the side seams. That way, you can stitch up the side seam and down the sleeve all in one.

12 FINISHING TOUCHES
Hems, buttons, buttonholes, hooks, eyes, press studs and under stitching the facings at shoulder seams are all done when the garment is all but finished.

Try this...
Aim to make your piece look every bit as good from the inside as the outside. This is not just for the glowing feeling of a job well done: it's because the neater the finish, the better the whole garment looks and hangs.

TACKING

Tacking, or basting as it's sometimes known, is making temporary stitches to hold pieces of fabric together before and during machine stitching. There are two purposes: first, to secure the pieces so that you can make sure they fit together well and lie flat before offering them to the machine; and second, to temporarily hold a garment together for fitting purposes. As you become a more experienced stitcher, you may not need to tack absolutely everything, depending on the fabric and complexity of the situation. Pins put in at right angles to the seamline (so that the machine can run over them) can suffice if you have a long, straight seam and you're using a stable fabric, such as cotton. However, even the professionals prefer to tack if they are working with a stretchy or slippery fabric. It's also good to tack anything that is fiddly or tricky, such as putting in zips or sleeves, or stitching round curves. If it feels laborious, cheer yourself with the thought that it's a whole lot better than unpicking botched machining. Choose a contrasting thread for tacking – it's so much easier to see both whilst machining and removing it afterwards.

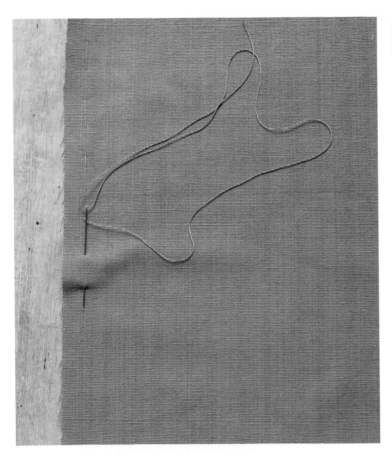

EVEN TACKING

The most basic and usual form of tacking that can be used in a variety of circumstances.

Using a contrast thread, thread a needle with a single strand and knot the end. Bring the needle up from the underside, then make what's essentially a line of long running stitches.

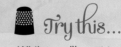 **Try this…**

Whilst you'll want to start off tacking using thread that has been knotted at the end, it's not always necessary to 'finish off' when you've finished, especially if you intend to machine the seam immediately. Then 'unpicking' the tacking once the seam has been stitched is just a matter of pulling the knotted end.

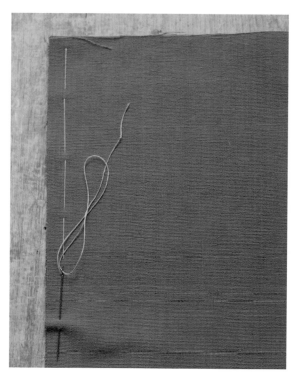

UNEVEN TACKING

This is a useful way to quickly tack long lengths, such as straight seams. It is similar to even tacking, except the stitches are longer and the gaps shorter. For a more secure version, alternate long stitches with short stitches.

Bring the needle up from the wrong side, tack a long stitch, pass the needle back down to the wrong side, bring it up to the right side, tack a stitch no longer than the needle length, back down and up again in a single action. Now allow a long stitch again before repeating the down-up-down-up procedure again.

DIAGONAL TACKING

This is used to secure layers of fabrics over larger areas – for example, to stitch the body of a lining or interlining on drapes or lapels. Not designed to be seen, diagonal tacking is always hidden in the structure of the garment or piece, keeping the fabric flat and stopping it from slithering about as you join the main pieces.

Tack parallel horizontal stitches at the back of the work to make long, even diagonal stitches at the front of the work.

HANDSTITCHES

Even if you're a dedicated machinist, there will be times when you need to finish off your work with hand stitches. The most useful and widely used are given here. None are difficult, but it takes practice before you'll automatically make stitches that are even both in length and tension.

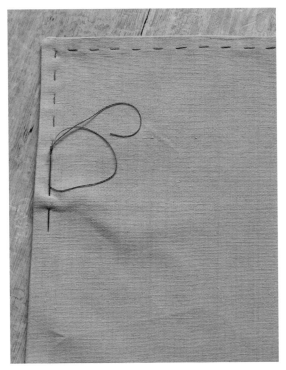

RUNNING STITCH

This is the simplest of stitches where you make a series of even stitches with even gaps. It is used as the basic stitch for hand gathering or easing.

Using a single strand of knotted thread, bring the needle through to the front from the underside of the fabric. Working from right to left (reverse this if you are left-handed), weave the needle in and out of the fabric, making both the stitches and the gaps between them the same length and taking several stitches onto the needle before drawing the thread through.

SADDLE STITCH

This is a smaller, neater version of running stitch. Sewn with the top, or right, side of the fabric facing upwards, it can be used as a hand-sewn topstitch to define edges.

Make neat stitches about 6mm (¼in) long with even gaps.

BACKSTITCH

Backstitch is the standard stitch that was generally used for seams in pre-sewing-machine days. It's still a good standby for small areas that are tricky to get to on the machine.

Using a single strand of knotted thread, bring the needle through to the front from the underside of the fabric. Make one running stitch. Now take the thread back to the end of the first running stitch, along the wrong side of the fabric and up again by the same length as the first stitch. Pull out any slack. Now go back to the point where the thread came out previously. As you work along the seam in this way, you will see that you have made what looks like a line of machine stitches. If you turn the fabric over to the wrong side, it won't look so neat as the stitches overlap each other. But the result is robust.

47

Try this…

If the two edges need a little easing, instead of holding them together as shown in the photograph, wrap them around your hand to take up a little slack where needed, then work the stitches.

EVEN SLIPSTITCH

This is one of the most useful finishing stitches to learn. It is used to join two folded edges – for example, where you are closing the opening in a seam in an item that has been turned through. The idea is that you hide as much of the stitch inside the foldlines of the fabric.

1 Pass the needle from the inside of the fold to the front, take a tiny stitch into the opposite fold, pass the needle along inside the fold and bring it out to the front, then take a tiny stitch into the first fold and pass the needle along that first fold.

2 When you get to the end, take two tiny stitches on top of each other in a concealed place to finish. The result is strong, secure and neat.

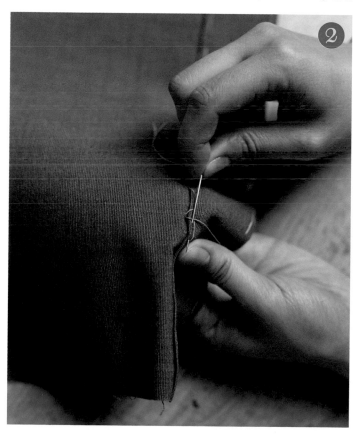

UNEVEN SLIPSTITCH

Uneven slipstitch makes a neat job of joining a folded edge to a single main piece of fabric, as in a double-fold hem. It's worked in a similar way to even slipstitch, but you can only run the needle along the inside of the single fold and you want to make as little impression on the front side of the main piece of fabric as possible.

(1) When you bring the needle up from the inside of the fold, just take a couple of threads from the main fabric.

(2) Next, bring the needle back to the fold and run it along the inside. Repeat along the length and finish with two tiny stitches on top of each other in a concealed place.

DOUBLE-FOLD HEM

A beautifully finished hem makes the difference to the overall look of a garment; but one that hangs perfectly evenly demands plenty of preparation. A double-fold hem is the dressmaking standard, encasing the raw edge and providing weight.

1 Start by turning the garment inside out and trimming the ends of the seams that will lie within the hem to reduce bulk. Next, give all the seams a firm press. Once you have established what length you want the garment to be, turn up and pin the hem near the fold. Check that it is lying straight, then tack close to the fold. Next, cut a length of card for the hem to the desired depth of the hem. Use this as a template to mark off the hem, allowing an extra 1cm (⅜in) for turning under, and trim off the excess. Press in 1cm (⅜in) all along the raw edge, then pin the hem in place.

2 Now tack another line of stitches along the top fold. If you are making an A-line skirt, you might find there is excess fabric at the top fold to accommodate. If this is the case, run a short line of easing stitches to help spread the excess.

3 Use uneven slipstitch to work the hem. Bring the needle up from inside the fold, then pick up two or three threads from the main fabric. Run the needle along the inside of the fold again, then bring it out and take another tiny stitch in the main fabric. Continue to the end of the hem.

SEWING SEAMS

Purists would say that every seam should be pinned, tacked and then stitched, and we have included those steps in all our instructions. However, as you become more adept with the sewing machine, this won't always be necessary. For example, when stitching simple straight seams on non-stretchy, non-slippery fabric, many dressmakers dispense with the tacking stage. Once you're confident enough to do this, you'll need to put the pins in across the seamline, rather than along it. That way, it's easy to remove the pins as you go, just before they reach the presser foot of your sewing machine. Curved seams, difficult-to-get-at corners or places where one piece of eased or gathered fabric is being stitched to a flat piece should be tacked before being offered to the more hurried 'jaws' of the sewing machine. It's better to invest the time up front than risk a snarl-up that takes ages to unpick and might even damage the fabric in the process. It's also a good idea to tack slippery or stretchy fabrics before you stitch them.

STRAIGHT SEAMS

Place the two pieces of fabric right sides together, aligning the raw edges, and pin across the seams at intervals of about 15cm (6in). Raise the presser foot. Place the fabric under the needle, 1cm (⅜in) from the top edge, aligning the raw edges with the seam allowance marker guidelines that are etched onto the needle plate of your sewing machine. Press the reverse stitch switch and stitch backwards to the top edge, then stitch forwards from there all along the seam. At the end, stitch back up the seam by about 1cm (⅜in) to finish. Press the seam open.

Try this...

To keep a straight line, don't be tempted to watch the needle as you stitch: instead, keep your eye on the edge of the fabric running along the seam allowance marker on the needle plate.

MAY MARTIN

51

CURVED SEAMS

Work in exactly the same way as you would a straight seam. The key is to keep your eye on the raw edge of the seam, making sure that it aligns with the seam allowance marker on the needle plate at all times. This will mean that you automatically turn the fabric smoothly with the curve to create an even seam allowance. Finally, press the seam open.

① **CLIPPING INWARD CURVES** – Seams that curve inwards need to be trimmed close to the seam and clipped using the points of sharp scissors. This allows the edge to curve inwards once the piece is turned right side out.

② **NOTCHING OUTWARD CURVES** – Outward curves should be notched, by carefully snipping out tiny triangles of fabric from the seam allowance, making sure you don't snip into the stitches. This stops the seam allowance form forming bulky gathers once the piece is turned right side out.

SEWING AROUND CORNERS

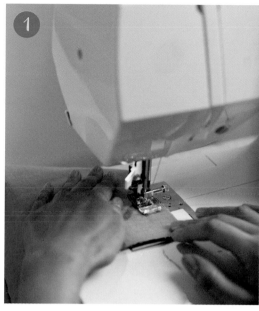

1 As well as seam allowance markers, most sewing machine needle plates have etched cross lines to help with accurate stitching around corners. If yours doesn't, stick masking tape across the needle plate in front of the needle at the standard seam allowance position of 1.5cm (⅝in). Stitch down one side of the corner in the same way as you would a straight seam until the needle is level with the masking-tape marker. Leave the needle in the down position.

2 Lift the presser foot, swivel the fabric around until the new edge aligns with the etched seamline on the needle plate or with your own masking-tape marker.

3 Lower the presser foot and stitch down the new seam.

FINISHING SEAMS

Any seams that are not enclosed need to be finished to neaten them and stop the fabric from fraying. There are several ways to do this: which one will depend on the fabric, the capability of your machine and speed.

PINKING

This is the quickest and simplest way to finish seams and a good solution unless you have a fabric that frays really readily, as the pinked edges would soon become eroded. Trim the seam allowance as close to the edge as possible. On finer fabrics, you can cut both layers at once. For thicker fabrics, press the seam open, then pink one side at a time.

TURNING IN

Turn in and press 6mm (¼in) to the wrong side. Set the machine to straight stitch – and stitch. This is quick, easy and can be done on the same machine without changing the settings. Even an antique sewing machine could cope with this one.

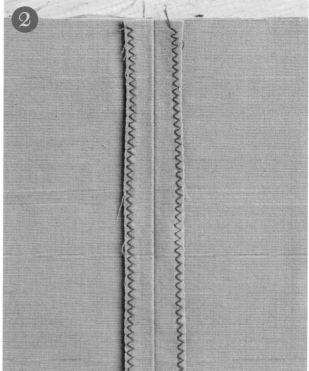

(1) Set the machine to a medium-width short zigzag stitch, then stitch down one seam allowance as close to the raw edge as possible. Make sure only the seam allowance is under the needle. When you've completed one side, turn the piece around so only the other seam allowance is under the needle.

(2) Trim to neaten if you wish, taking care not to cut through any stitches. The finished seams are now both neat and flatter than turned-in finishing.

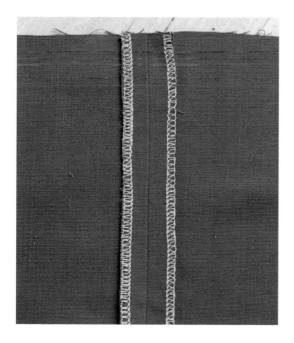

OVERLOCKING

This professional-looking finish can only be achieved using an overlocker, which is a separate and not inexpensive machine. It trims and finishes the seams in a single action and is sometimes even used to stitch the seams at the same time. However, as it cuts the fabric as it sews, amateurs can sometimes find they've cut into the main body of the garment at the same time, thereby ruining their work. If you do decide to invest in one, you can safeguard damaging your work by finishing the seams with the overlocker before, rather than after, sewing them.

ENCLOSED SEAMS

Some garments need to be made using enclosed seams, where the raw edges of a first seam are enclosed within a second. These are usually used on items made of fine fabric worn close to the body, such as lingerie, or, at the other end of the scale, on hard-wearing workwear such as jeans.

FRENCH SEAMS

Lingerie, made from fine fabrics that are in constant contact with the skin, is usually made using French seams, which are strong, surprisingly hard-wearing and look almost as good on the inside of the garment as on the outside.

① With wrong sides together, pin and stitch the seam 5mm (¼in) from the raw edge. Trim the seam to 3mm (⅛in) and press open.

② Turn the seam through so that the right sides are together, fold along the seamline and press. Tack as close as you can to the first seam.

③ Machine stitch, stitching 1cm (⅜in) in from the seamed edge, enclosing the raw edges, and reverse stitching at each end to secure. Press the seam to one side.

④ Finally, pull out the tacking stitches. This will be easy if the stitching line sits just outside the tacking – if the machined stitches encroach on the tacking, it's far more fiddly.

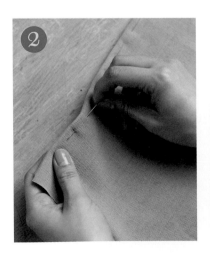

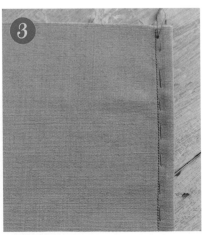

FLAT FELL SEAMS

These are typically used on jeans. They are very robust, yet flat on the inside, so they don't rub the skin.

1 With wrong sides together, stitch a plain seam 1.5cm (⅝in) from the raw edge, using a topstitching thread. Press the seam open and then press both seam allowances towards the back of the garment. Trim the underneath layer to 3mm (⅛in).

2 On the untrimmed seam allowance, press 3mm (⅛in) to the wrong side, then press this over the trimmed raw edge. Pin in position, placing the pins across the seam. Topstitch as close to the folded edge as possible.

TRIMMING SEAMS

When a seam will not be visible because it is turned through and enclosed, for example a collar, a facing or a cushion cover, it must be trimmed. Otherwise the resulting seam will be bulky and won't lie flat. There are several ways to do this.

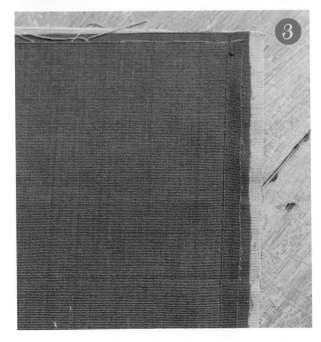

GRADING

It's especially important to reduce bulk when you are using heavy fabric, or where several layers are being joined (such as where the body of the garment and facings meet in several layers at the shoulder seams). To do this, you need to trim the seam allowances to different widths.

1. First, neaten the seams by trimming 6mm (¼in) off all layers. Then, leaving the lowest layer, trim a little off the edge of the next layer.

2. Now trim a larger margin from the layer above that.

3. When all the layers have been trimmed to different margins, the seam allowance lies flatter.

EXTERNAL CORNERS

Always snip off corners before turning them through. Cut close to the stitches, but be careful not to snip into them. Where there is a particularly sharp point, start by cutting off the corner, then taper the sides to reduce the bulk. This will make for a neater point once it is turned through.

INTERNAL CORNERS

To reduce bulk at internal corners, place a pin at the corner, just inside the line of stitching at the corner, then snip into it with sharp scissors. That way, you can be sure that you don't cut the stitches by mistake.

SHAPING AND CONTOURING

The art of dressmaking is transforming flat pieces of fabric into three-dimensional garments that fit the contours of the body. But even the simplest of garments relies on more than just joining straight seams. There are several ways to create shape: by using darts, gathers and contoured seams.

SINGLE-POINT DARTS

Plain or single-point darts are the most commonly used, predominantly to shape the waists of skirts and trousers. Whenever you sew a dart, always press the dart in the direction specified using lots of steam.

(1) With right sides together, match the dots at the widest part of the dart to make a fold that reaches down to the single point at the end of the dart. Pin and hand tack just inside the stitch line. Machine stitch from the widest end of the dart to the point, then make two more stitches right on the fold to make a crisp, clean point.

(2) To finish, tie the two ends of thread together in a knot at the tip of the dart and then remove the tacking stitches.

CONTOUR DARTS

Sometimes called double-point darts, contour darts are designed to nip in fabric on dresses – at waistlines, for example. Marked up on the flat fabric, you're likely to have an elongated diamond shape with a point at each end – hence the name.

(1) Match the markers right sides together at the widest points of the diamond shape and pin across the fold. In the same way, pin across the fold at intervals until you reach the single top marker. Repeat towards the bottom marker. Tack just inside the stitch line.

(2) Starting at the widest point, stitch just inside the tacking towards the top point of the dart. Return to the widest point again and stitch towards the bottom of the dart in the same way. Tie the pairs of threads together at the widest point and the points at each end.

(3) The widest part will need to be clipped. Protect the stitches at the point by placing a pin just inside the stitch line before clipping with sharp scissors.

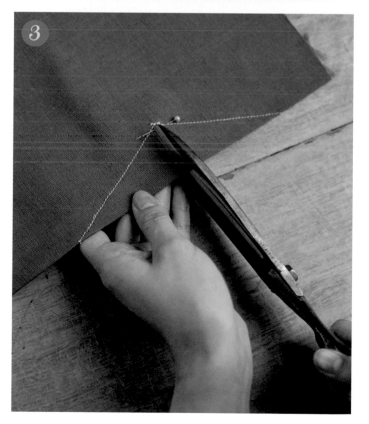

HAND GATHERING

Easy and fun, this is a simple first sewing skill to learn. As the gathering stitches are usually later enclosed into a waistband or otherwise hidden, there is less demand for perfection than with other skills – although it has to be said, the more even the gathering stitches, the easier it is to manage the next stage of stitching on the bodice or waistband and the better the end result.

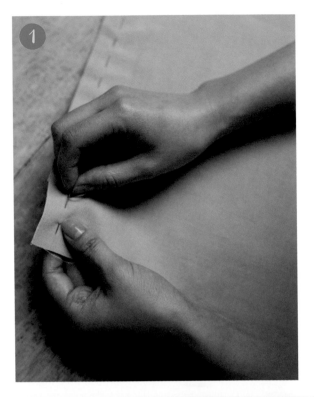

(1) Using contrast thread, make a large knot in one end then make a line of running stitches along the raw edge to be gathered. Ideally, the thread you're using should be at least as long as the edge to be gathered. This is not always possible. A full dirndl skirt, for example, may have such full gathers that the length of thread would be almost impossible to handle without getting tangled. In this case, divide off the length to be gathered into quarters and work four equal lengths of gathers.

(2) When the line is complete, pull up the gathers to the desired length. Wind the spare pulled-up thread around a pin placed at the end of the line of gathers. That way, the gathers are stabilised while you even them out along the line. If, once you've pinned the gathered edge to the straight piece (waistband or bodice for example), you find you've not pulled it up quite enough, or too much, perhaps, you can unwind the spare thread from the pin, adjust and re-wind.

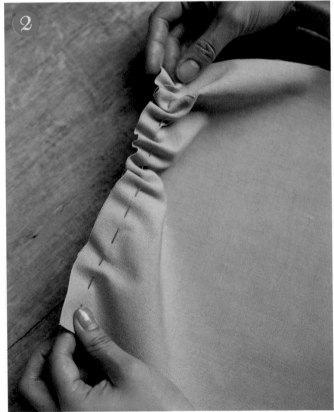

GATHERING AND EASING

Gathering and easing both add fullness to the fabric, bringing three-dimensional shape to two-dimensional fabric without the need for darts.

EASING

Easing can be used where two pieces of fabric that are slightly different in length need to be joined. By easing, you can ensure that the ends align, as any slack can be taken up all along the length of the longer piece rather than bunched up at the end. Easing is also used to create shape at the top of a sleeve, for example. As the sleeve top is cut in a curve and is slightly larger than the armhole, when the easing is pulled up, it provides a 'shell' that curves over the natural curve of the shoulder. Easing lines are often made over only a part of the length of the seam and a commercial pattern will be marked with circles or dots to show where the easing should begin and end.

Run two lines of small running stitches between the markers. Place a pin at each end for easy adjustment, then pull up in the same way as gathering stitches (see opposite).

Try this...

Avoid the bunched look on hemlines that widen towards the bottom, such as A-line skirts and flared trousers by running a line of easing gathers. That way, the excess fabric can be spread evenly over the whole hemline before stitching.

INSERTING ZIPS

The most versatile of all fastenings, zips are used not just in garments but also soft furnishings, such as loose sofa or chair covers. As well as being a neat and practical way of getting in and out of garments, zips have, in themselves, become a fashion statement. Sometimes zips are invisible, hidden neatly away in the seam allowance, but they can also be 'revealed' and as much a part of the project design as any trimming. The most usual insertion technique is the centred zip but other methods are the lapped zip, often used for the fly of a pair of trousers. However, putting in a zip neatly takes practice and some methods are easier than others. The trick is to take your time and to pin and tack at every stage. You will need an ordinary zip foot for most zips, which should come as part of your machine's tool kit.

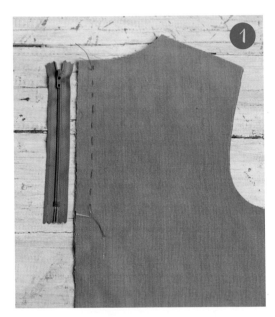

CENTRED ZIP

This is the traditional method of choice for centre back zips (on dresses for example) before the advent of invisible zips. It is also the easiest to put in, and very versatile, so a good choice for beginners.

① Start by using the zip itself to measure the opening. Align the top of the tapes with the top raw edge of the garment, and place a pin on the garment seam allowance in the position of the zip's end stop. Now, tack using contrast thread, from this point down to the hemline, then machine stitch. Tack from the pin up towards the top raw edge of the garment. Press the seam open along its length.

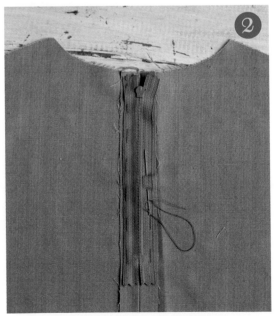

② Now place the zip face down on top of the seam allowance, with the teeth centred over the seam line and the raw edges of the tape meeting the top raw edges of the garment. Pin in position. Starting at the bottom, tack through all layers up one side to the top. Now tack through all layers on the other side, working in the same way from the bottom to the top. By working from the bottom to the top on both sides, rather than tacking all round, the fabric will lie flatter. Turn the piece over to check that the tacking is even on both sides of the zip on the right sides.

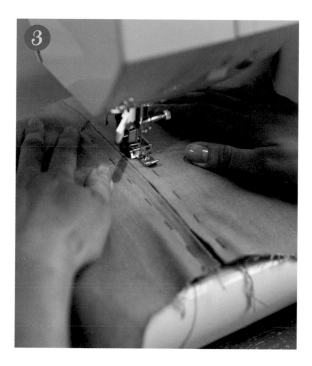

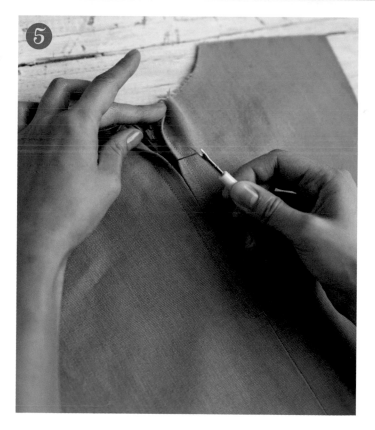

3 Fit a zip foot, then place the piece with the bottom end of the zip right sides up under the needle. Stitch up one side just outside the tacking stitches. Finish by reverse stitching at the top, then re-position the piece with the needle at the bottom again. Stitch from the first line of stitches, across the bottom, then up the other side just outside the tacking stitches. Reverse stitch to finish.

4 Now pull out the stitches tacking the zip in position. If you kept the stitch line just outside the tacking, this will be easy.

5 Finally, unpick the line of tacking that temporarily joined the seam. Using a hand sewing needle, thread up the loose end at one side of the end of the zip and pass through to the wrong side. Secure with several tiny stitches on top of each other. Repeat on the other side.

LAPPED ZIP

Traditionally used for side zips in skirts and dresses, the lap should lie towards the back, giving a smooth line to the garment.

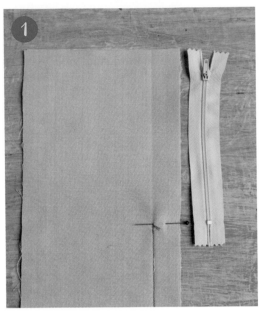

(1) Start by using the zip itself to measure the opening. Align the top of the tapes with the top raw edge of the garment, and place a pin in the garment seam allowance at the position of the teeth end stop. Pin, tack and stitch down from this to the hemline. Press the whole seam open, including the unstitched part.

(2) With right sides down, now press open a further 6mm (¼in) on the left-hand side.

(3) Turn the piece over so the wrong sides are facing down. Fit a zip foot to the machine. Close the zip and position it under the pressed-back fold. Pin, tack and stitch. When you get near the slider, leave the needle down, pull the slider to the part you've already stitched and stitch to the end.

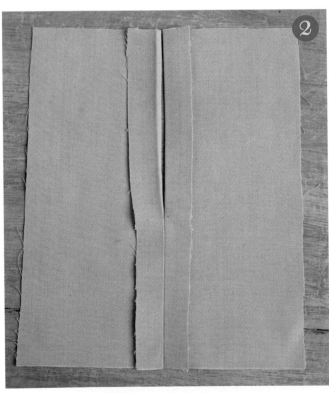

4 Lay the piece wrong sides down on a flat surface and pin the fold of the unstitched side of fabric over the stitched side. Using contrast thread, tack along the bottom and up the unstitched side as far away from the teeth as possible, catching all layers.

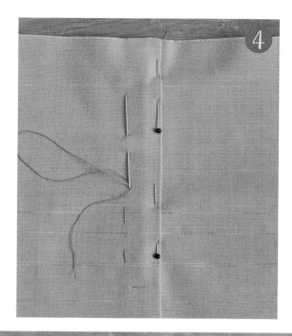

5 Now place masking tape over the tacking stitches. This acts as a straight guide for stitching and also stops you from stitching over the tacking stitches. Stitch across the bottom first, then up to the top. Peel off the masking tape.

6 For a neat finish, thread the loose machine thread at the end of the zip onto a hand needle and pass the thread to the back. Use several small stitches on top of each other within the seam allowance at the wrong sides to secure.

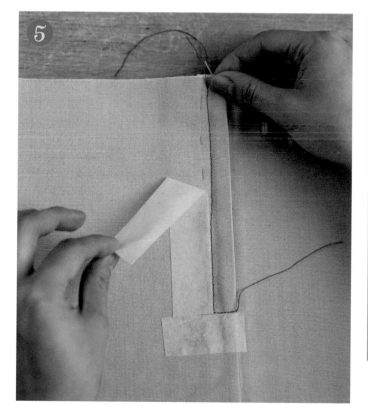

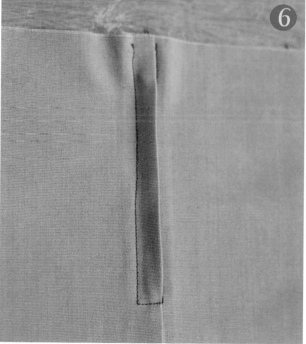

INVISIBLE ZIP

For an invisible zip, you need a special invisible zip foot that allows you to stitch under the nylon coil. This doesn't come as part of the basic kit for most sewing machines so will need to be bought separately. Invisible zips can be tricky to put in, but with practice, you'll get the knack. Once they're hidden in the seamline, invisible zips give a smart, tailored finish. While other zips are stitched in from the bottom up, invisible zips need to be stitched from the top down; for this reason, many people like to leave stitching the rest of the seam until after they have put in the zip, rather than before, which can leave an awkward bubble at the end of the zip.

1 Run a line of contrast tacking stitches along the seamlines of both pieces of fabric for the length of the zip opening. Open the zip and use a very cool iron to press the ridge of the coil over to the front sides of the tapes on both sides. Close the zip and lay it face down over the tacking on one side, aligning the top raw edges of the tapes with the top raw edges of the garment. Pin and tack in position.

2 Open the zip and, starting at the top and making sure the coil is under the right groove on the invisible zip foot, stitch down the length of the zip. Close the zip. Aligning the top raw edges of the zip tape with the top raw edges of the garment, pin and tack the zip over the line of tacking on the other piece of fabric.

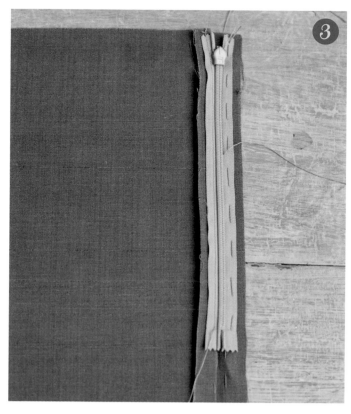

Try this...

Take your time over zips and never cut corners on pinning and tacking. The more accurately the zip is put in, the easier you'll find neatly joining the next pieces. A well put in zip makes a huge difference to the overall look of the whole garment.

MAY MARTIN

3) Open the zip again, then stitch it to the single layer of the other side, using the same method as you did the first side. Tack the lower part of the seam and stitch from the end of the zip to the hemline. Finally, press the seam open and thoroughly press the newly stitched-in invisible zip.

4) Once the zip has been inserted, use a good shot of steam to press the garment on the right side. This will neaten the zip, settle it into position and really flatten the piece before you move onto the next stage.

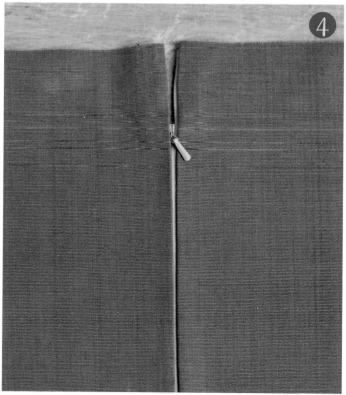

BIAS BINDING

Bias binding can be used to neaten seams or hems, to trim edges and can be made into ties. Cut on the bias, its natural stretch means that it happily goes around corners, neatly lying flat, and for this reason, it is often used to trim necklines. It can be bought ready cut and folded, in myriad colours and widths, but making your own is a useful skill. The key is to make sure the fabric is cut at a perfect 45-degree angle to the selvedge to even widths along its length.

MAKING BIAS BINDING

(1) The 45-degree line is not difficult to manage. Simply pull out a thread running between the selvedges and cut along the line it creates. Now fold this down until it matches the selvedge. Press hard on the fold to create a crease, as this will be the first 45-degree line. Cut along the creased fold. Then, using a ruler, measure out the desired width of the bias – a useful standard is 6cm (2½in wide) at regular intervals along the length of the crease and draw in the first line parallel to the creased fold. Repeat several times until you have measured out enough length of bias for your desired project. Cut out the lengths of bias as accurately as you can. Scissors are fine, but you may find you can get more accurate cuts using a quilter's rotary cutter and ruler.

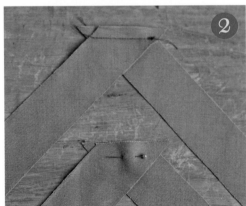

(2) Now the lengths need to be stitched together. As they have been cut on the bias along the full length of the fabric, each one will have a 45-degree end. Place two pieces right sides together so that the long edges meet, creating a V-shape with little points at the end. Pin. Open out the piece to check you now have a long, straight piece of bias. If you don't, you've matched up the pieces wrongly – so try again! Once you are satisfied the pieces are pinned together properly, stitch. Snip off the points.

(3) Press the seams open, then press the raw edges to the middle all along the length of the bias.

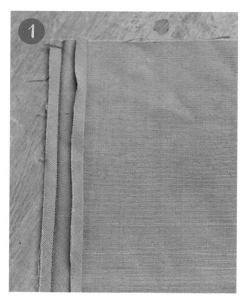

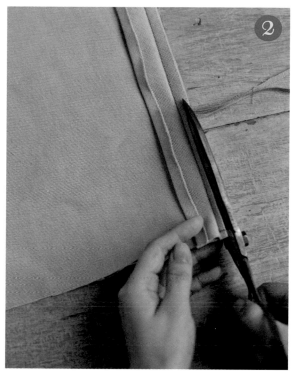

APPLYING BIAS BINDING

(1) With right sides together, match one long raw edge of the bias binding with the edge to be bound. Pin in position, placing the pins at right angles to the raw edges. Stitch in the fold along the length of the bias, then remove the pins.

(2) Now trim the seam close to the line of stitching and turn the bias binding to the wrong side along the stitch line, with the raw edge folded under along the crease line.

(3) Hand stitch the bias to the wrong side using slipstitch. Alternatively, turn the bias to the wrong side, tack it over the original line of stitching, then machine it into position, keeping as close as possible to the folded edge. This is trickier than hand stitching; unless you're an accurate machinist, you could end up with uneven stitching.

MAKING BUTTONHOLES

Badly stitched buttonholes can ruin a garment and getting them right takes a lot of practice. Thankfully, nowadays even the most basic sewing machine has a buttonhole setting. Less sophisticated machines have one that involves four steps consisting of close zigzag stitches along the length of the buttonhole and a bar tack at each end. More sophisticated computerised machines have a special foot that can memorise the size of a button and then automatically stitch the right-sized buttonhole in one easy step. Practise several times on spare fabric until you are confident in your machining skills and sure the tension is absolutely correct. Make sure the test buttonholes are an accurate representation of the finished ones by using the same thread and layering up all the relevant fabrics, including facings, linings and interlinings.

① Start by marking the buttonhole positions. Many patterns have these printed in position and all you have to do is transfer the markings. If not, decide where the buttonholes should be. Measure out the positions carefully from the sewn edge to either end of each buttonhole and measure the distance from the hem upwards to each end to make sure they are straight, evenly placed and correctly positioned. Mark using tailor's chalk. Check the length of the buttonhole by placing the button on top of the mark. It should be fractionally longer than the diameter of the button – by the same amount as the depth of the button.

② If you are making a four-step buttonhole, set the machine at the first buttonhole position and stitch along the top of the buttonhole. Adjust the dial to stitch the end bar. Adjust it again to stitch along the lower edge of the buttonhole, and finally, adjust for the other end bar. Place a pin at either end of the buttonhole just inside the end bars and snip between the pins using sharp embroidery scissors.

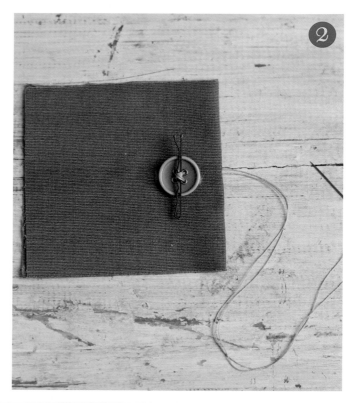

ADDING BUTTONS

(1) Mark the button positions in the corresponding positions to the buttonholes, carefully measuring in the same way as you did for the buttonholes. Mark with tailor's chalk.

(2) Hold the button in position and, using double thread knotted at the end, bring the needle up from under the fabric through the first hole in the button. Provide a little slack in the stitches by putting a hairgrip or match across the button and sew over it into the next hole. Continue in this way, making a cross of stitches if it's a four-hole button.

(3) Remove the hairgrip or match and create a thread stalk by winding the thread between the button and the fabric. Finally, pass the needle through to the wrong side and make a series of tiny stitches on top of each other at the back to secure.

THE
PROJECTS

MAKING THE PROJECTS

The collection of projects in this section has been designed to provide you with the core skills needed to make almost anything you might want to sew. With the exception of two of the contestant's garments made for challenges set as part of *The Great British Sewing Bee* – the Summer Dress and the Hacking Jacket – each of the projects has been designed with the beginner sewer in mind. There's projects to make for the home, wardrobe staples and one off pieces. The step-by-step instructions have been written and illustrated so that, depending on your skill level, they can be read in different ways – either at-a-glance or more in-depth.

Using the patterns

With the exception of the Button-Back Blouse on pages 90–95, which is not available to download, there are three ways to get your pattern pieces for each garment.

DOWNLOAD go to www.quadrille.co.uk/sewingbee/patterns. You'll be able to download all the patterns from the dedicated web page. The pattern pieces come as print-and-tile sheets, which means they can be printed out on a home printer on A4 paper that can be stuck together like tiles.

PHOTOCOPY take the book to a photocopy shop where you can have the individual pattern pages copied, enlarging them by the percentage given to provide full-size patterns.

SCALE UP for this you'll need dressmaker's squared paper, which is marked with 1cm and 5cm squares. Each small graph square on the gridded patterns in the book represents 1cm square on the dressmaker's paper so the lines can be transferred.

Skill levels and project difficulty ratings

The different sections of the book have been designed to work together to make the projects easy to follow for an absolute beginner and sewing enthusiasts alike.

✎ ABSOLUTE BEGINNERS are best advised to start with a project with a one-button difficulty rating. The projects are accompanied with fully illustrated step-by-step instructions, but beginners who are not familiar with key sewing terms can refer to the detailed explanations of the various techniques in the Basic Sewing Skills section. Start with one-button projects.

✎ SEWERS WITH BASIC SEWING SKILLS who are familiar with general sewing terms should be able to follow the full project instructions in conjunction with the illustrations. Look out for one-, two-, three- and four-button projects.

✎ SEASONED STITCHERS who are experienced and adept at sewing may not need to read the full project instructions, but be able to follow the at-a-glance step headings and illustrations. Choose from any of the projects, regardless of its button rating.

Choosing the right size

All the garments in the book are given in UK women's sizes 8 to 16, with the exception of the pyjama trousers which come in four unisex sizes and the waistcoat, which comes in men's sizes.

UK size	8	10	12	14	16
US size	6	8	10	12	14
EUR size	34	36	38	40	42
Bust	80cm 31½in	83cm 32½in	87cm 34in	92cm 36in	97cm 38in
Waist	61cm 24in	64cm 25in	67cm 26½in	71cm 28in	76cm 30in
Hip	85cm 33½in	88cm 34½in	92cm 36in	97cm 38in	102cm 40in
Neck to waist	40cm 15½in	40.5cm 16in	41.5cm 16½in	42cm 16½in	42.5cm 16½in

Difficulty ratings

Each project has been given a difficulty rating indicated by button icons.

⊞ ⊞ ⊞ ⊞ ⊞ – straight and curved seams only: best choice for beginners

⊞ ⊞ ⊞ ⊞ ⊞ – both straight and curved seams, inserting zips

⊞ ⊞ ⊞ ⊞ ⊞ – straight and curved seams, inserting zips, easing fabric

⊞ ⊞ ⊞ ⊞ ⊞ – all of the above, but with more individual pattern pieces

⊞ ⊞ ⊞ ⊞ ⊞ – the trickier projects requiring some basic tailoring such as linings, interlinings and precision pressing

TUNIC

A classic wardrobe staple, the sleeveless tunic is a versatile item of clothing that can be made from just over a metre of fabric. It is easy to make if you decide on a cotton fabric. If you're more experienced try it in a soft washed silk, like the version shown here.

DIFFICULTY RATING: ⊞ ⊞ ⊞ ⊞ ⊞

The simple tunic has been with us since the Roman tunica, and has never been out of fashion. It's been designed so you can make a flattering long-line top, like the one shown here, a shorter version that would look good with fitted skirts, trousers or jeans, or, by cutting it longer, a fun young 1960s-style mini dress.

TUNIC SIZES
To fit UK women's sizes 8, 10, 12, 14 and 16.
The finished lengths of the tunic range from approximately 54cm (21in) for the short-line top, 73cm (29in) for the long-line top to 82cm (32in) for the mini dress, but the length is easily adjustable.

FABRIC FINDER
The exquisite coral tones of this washed silk have a vintage-style bloom that lends elegance to the garment. The soft flowing drape skims the bumpy bits whilst flattering the curves.
Try these alternatives:
Silk crepe de Chine—Laundered fine cotton—Silk-rayon—Cotton jersey—Voile

Materials
1.4m (1½yd) of 140cm-
  (55in-) wide washed
  silk or 1.7m (2yd)
  of 115cm- (45in-)
  wide fabric
Complementary or
  contrasting nylon zip,
  50cm (20in) long
Matching sewing thread

SKILLS SET
Working even slipstitch see page 48—Slipstitching double-fold hems see page 50
Stitching straight seams see page 51—Clipping curved seams see page 52
Finishing seams see pages 54 and 55—Stitching single-point darts see page 60

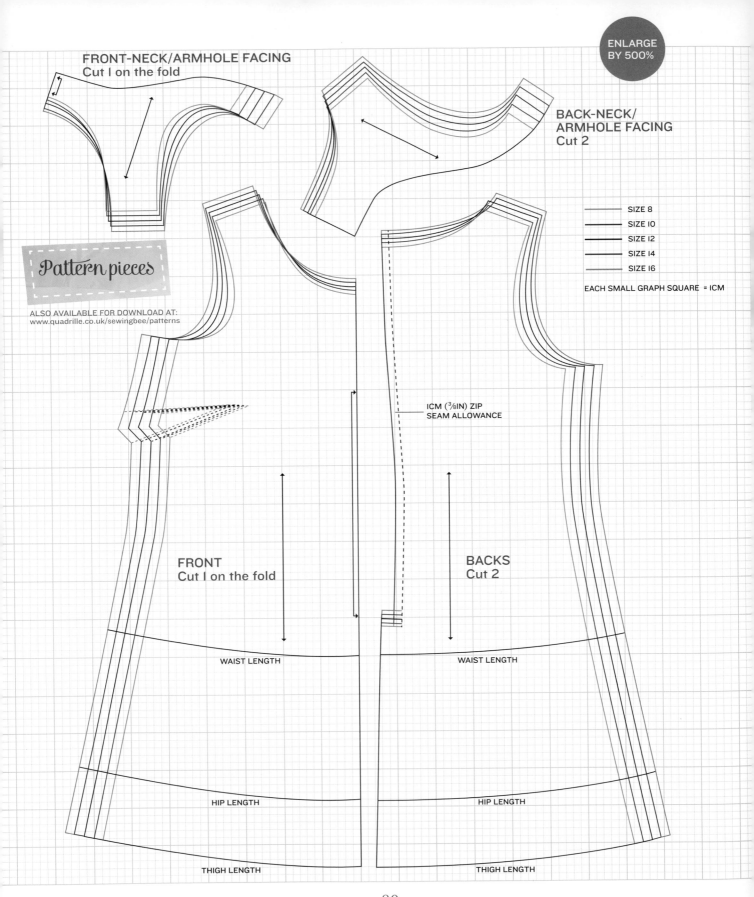

FRONT-NECK/ARMHOLE FACING
Cut I on the fold

BACK-NECK/ARMHOLE FACING
Cut 2

ENLARGE
BY 500%

SIZE 8
SIZE 10
SIZE 12
SIZE 14
SIZE 16

EACH SMALL GRAPH SQUARE = ICM

ICM (⅜IN) ZIP
SEAM ALLOWANCE

FRONT
Cut I on the fold

BACKS
Cut 2

WAIST LENGTH

WAIST LENGTH

HIP LENGTH

HIP LENGTH

THIGH LENGTH

THIGH LENGTH

Cutting diagram

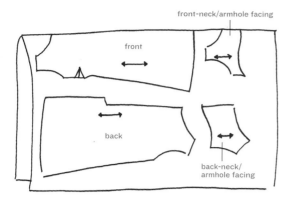

front-neck/armhole facing

front

back

back-neck/
armhole facing

Cutting guide

Press the fabric thoroughly before cutting.

FROM THE FABRIC:

✂ Cut one tunic front and one front-neck/
armhole facing, each on the fold.

✂ Cut two tunic backs and two back-neck/
armhole facings.

The 1.5cm (⅝in) seam allowances and a 2cm
(¾in) hem allowance are included in these
pieces, as well as the 1cm (⅜in) zip opening
turnbacks. (If you want a slightly longer or
shorter skirt, take this into account when cutting
the front and backs.)

To make the tunic

1 STITCH THE BACK PIECES TOGETHER
With right sides together, pin the tunic back pieces together.
Use the zip to measure down the back seam and mark the end
stop with a pin. Tack from the pin down to the hem and stitch,
taking a 1.5cm (⅝in) seam allowance and leaving the zip section
open. Note that the seam allowance along the zip opening is only
1cm (⅜in). Finish the raw seam edges and press the seam open.

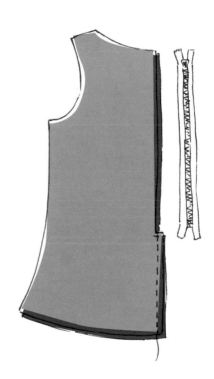

2 INSERT THE ZIP
Insert a revealed zip so that the zip tape
is visible on the right side of the back, folding
under the 1cm (⅜in) seam allowance all around
the zip.

3 STITCH THE DARTS
Carefully stitch the single-point darts on the tunic front.

Try this...
The method used for sewing the all-in-one neck/armhole facing to the tunic top is a little tricky, but it is especially suitable for silk – as all the raw seam edges are hidden inside the facing. If you are using a crisp cotton fabric for the tunic, why not try the easier method of adding the facing used for the Basic Dress on pages 210–212.

4 STITCH THE FRONT TO THE BACK
With right sides together, stitch the side seams. Finish the seam edges and press the seams open.

5 FINISH THE BOTTOM EDGE OF THE FACING
On each facing piece, press 6mm (¼in) to the wrong side along the bottom edge of the facing, pin and stitch.

6 STITCH THE FACING AROUND THE NECK EDGE AND ARMHOLES

With right sides together, pin, tack and stitch the facing to the tunic around the neckline and around the armholes. Trim close to the stitching, clip the curves and press the seams open. Turn the tunic right side out.

7 FINISH THE FACING SEAMS AND SHOULDER SEAMS

At the side seams of the facings, turn in the seam allowance and slip stitch together along the folds. Repeat with the shoulder seams.

8 SLIPSTITCH THE FACING ALONG THE ZIP

At the zip edges, turn in the raw edges of the facing and slipstitch to the zip tape.

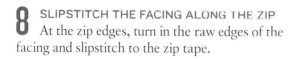

9 HEM THE TUNIC TOP

For a quick hem, machine stitch it neatly in place. At the hem edge, turn up 1cm (⅜in) twice, press and tack. Machine stitch this double hem, stitching close to the first fold.

PYJAMA TROUSERS

*An easy project for a starter sewer.
Make these drawstring trousers in a fine
seersucker, like those shown here, or a warm
fleece for cosy nights and you have a great pair of
trousers suitable both for girls and boys.*

DIFFICULTY RATING:

Materials

2.5m (3yd) of striped
cotton fabric, 115cm
(45in) wide
2m (2yd) of contrasting
cotton pyjama tape,
1.5cm (⅝in) wide
Matching sewing thread

Pyjama trousers are the easiest ever garment to make and to
wear. Loose and slouchy, there's no tricky fitting and no fiddly
fastenings – when it comes to putting them on, just tighten the
tape ties that run around the waistband low on the hips. Learning
how to make a drawstring channel for ties is a useful skill for
accessories and homewares as well as garments. Although there
is one curved seam to sew, it isn't a tightly fitting seam. Basic
drawstring pyjama trousers are a great choice for a first make
because you really can't go wrong.

PYJAMA SIZES
Unisex sizes S, M, L and XL.

FABRIC FINDER
Pyjama trousers are all about comfort. Natural fibres are best
as they absorb moisture, are breatheable and are pleasant to the
touch. Fine seersucker is an excellent summer choice as the crinkles
keep the fabric away from the skin for a fabulously cool feel.
Try these alternatives:
**Soft fine cotton—Brushed cotton—Cotton flannel—Seersucker—
Flannelette—Cotton jersey**

SKILLS SET
Slipstitching double-fold hems see page 50
Stitching straight seams see page 51—Clipping curved seams see page 52
Finishing seams see pages 54 and 55—Making buttonholes see page 72

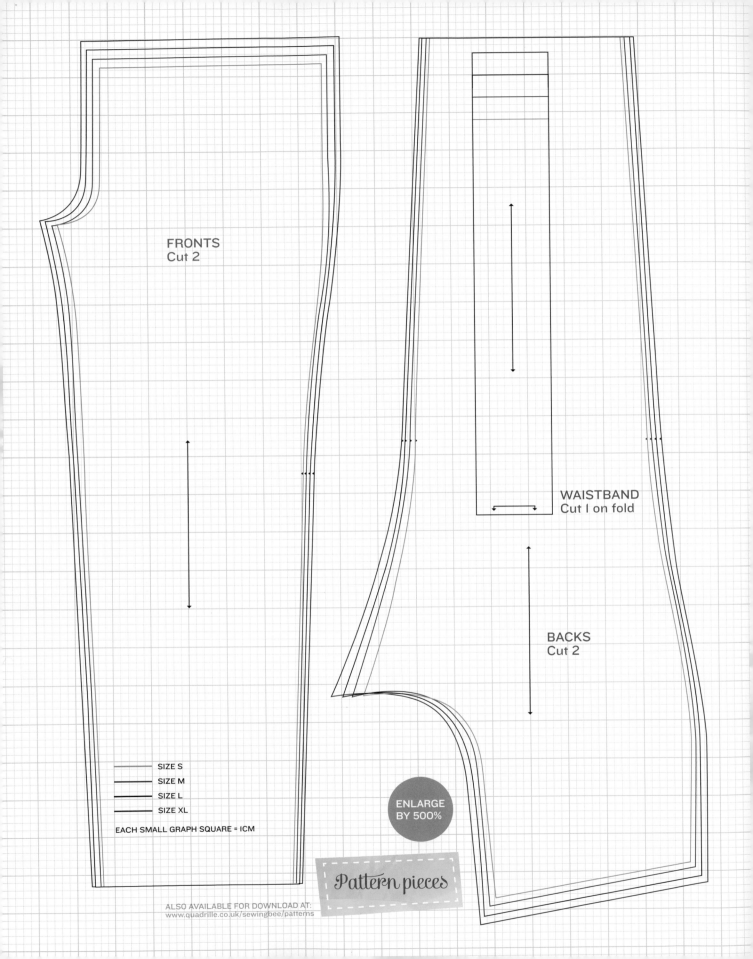

FRONTS
Cut 2

WAISTBAND
Cut 1 on fold

BACKS
Cut 2

SIZE S
SIZE M
SIZE L
SIZE XL

EACH SMALL GRAPH SQUARE = 1CM

ENLARGE
BY 500%

Pattern pieces

Cutting diagrams

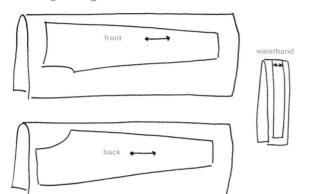

Cutting guide

Press the fabric carefully before cutting. Precisely cut curves help to make stitching easier.

FROM THE FABRIC:

✂ Cut two trouser fronts and two trouser backs.

✂ Cut one waistband, on the fold.

A 1.5cm (⅝in) seam allowance is included on all the pattern pieces, and a 3cm (1¼in) hem allowance on the bottom edges of the trouser fronts and backs.

To make the pyjama trousers

1 STITCH THE INNER LEG SEAMS

With right sides together, stitch one trouser back piece to the corresponding trouser front piece along the inside leg seam. Repeat with the other trouser back and front pieces. Finish the raw seam edges and press the seams open.

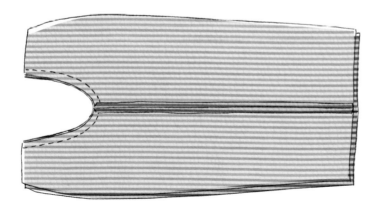

2 STITCH THE CENTRE SEAM

Now join the two legs together at the curved centre seam. With right sides together, stitch the centre seam from waist edge to waist edge. Now re-stitch this seam on top of the first line of stitching to strengthen the seam. Press the seam open, then press to one side. Finish the seam by using zigzag stitch through both layers to further strengthen the seam.

3 STITCH THE OUTER SIDE SEAMS
With right sides together, pin the front of the trousers to the back. Stitch. Finish the raw seam edges and press the seams open.

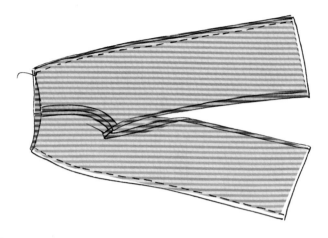

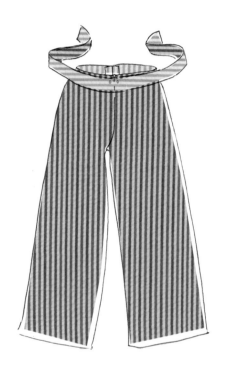

4 STITCH ON THE WAISTBAND
Fold the waistband in half widthways and mark the centre point with a pin. Mark two 12mm (½in) buttonhole positions, one 1.5cm (⅝in) either side of the pin and centred on the front section of the waistband – take into account the 1.5cm (⅝in) seam allowance on the waistband. Machine stitch the buttonholes. With right sides together, the raw edges aligned and the centre pin aligned with the centre front seam, pin the waistband onto the pyjamas. Where the ends of the waistband meet at the centre back, fold them under to align with the seamline and press. Place these ends right sides together and stitch along the fold. Trim and press the seam open. Pin the waistband back into position, tack in place and stitch 1.5cm (⅝in) from the edge. Press the seam and waistband upwards.

5 FINISH THE WAISTBAND
Press under 1.5cm (⅝in) along the free raw edge of the waistband. Pin this edge to the back of the waistband so it covers the line of stitching just completed. Tack then topstitch the waistband in place along the waistband seam.

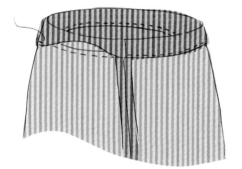

6 HEM THE TROUSERS AND ADD THE DRAWSTRING
Turn up 1.5cm (⅝in) twice around the bottom edges of the trouser legs to form a double hem. Press and tack. Stitch the hem close to the first fold. Lastly, thread the waistband tape through the waistband and hem the ends.

Try this...
The top of the stitching as you sew is always the better quality stitch. On areas where topstitching is used always work on the side of the garment that is going to show. MAY MARTIN

BUTTON-BACK BLOUSE

Fun, flattering and easy to sew, you'll want to make this button-back blouse over and over again. Create a completely different look by making the blouse in a glowing shade of plain silk for an elegant evening top or try making it in soft cotton lawn for warm summer days.

DIFFICULTY RATING:

This blouse, designed by one of *The Great British Sewing Bee* contestants, flatters any figure. It is also easy to make because the yoke is the only fitted part, so there's no fiddly pattern adjustment to worry about. However, the blouse has been given a three-button difficulty level because there are set-in sleeves. Nonetheless, it is an excellent project for a first-time sleeve setter because its relaxed design is more forgiving than a tailored piece. If you are a total beginner, you may also be worried about making the buttonholes. This shouldn't be too challenging if your machine has a buttonhole setting, but do try them out on spare fabric first. If you're not fully confident, sew on large snap fasteners instead and place buttons on top for the same effect.

BLOUSE SIZES
To fit UK women's sizes 8, 10, 12, 14 and 16.

FABRIC FINDER
The fullness of the bodice means that a softly draping lightweight fabric would be the most flattering choice.
Try these alternatives:
Silk or polyester crepe de Chine—Habotai—Charmeuse—
Soft cotton lawn—Chambray

Materials
- 1.6m (1¾yd) of fabric 115cm (45in) wide
- Matching sewing thread
- 50cm (20in) of contrasting narrow ready-made piping, for yoke decoration
- 40 x 50cm (16 x 20in) of lightweight iron-on interfacing
- Five 2cm (¾in) button moulds for covered buttons, or five 2cm (¾in) buttons
- Scrap of contrasting fabric (matching piping), to cover buttons (extra if making your own piping)

SKILLS SET
Stitching straight seams **see page 51**—Clipping curved seams **see page 52**
Stitching French seams **see page 56**—Sewing single-point darts **see page 60**
Hand gathering **see page 62**—Easing **see page 63**—Making buttonholes **see page 72**
Adding buttons **see page 73**

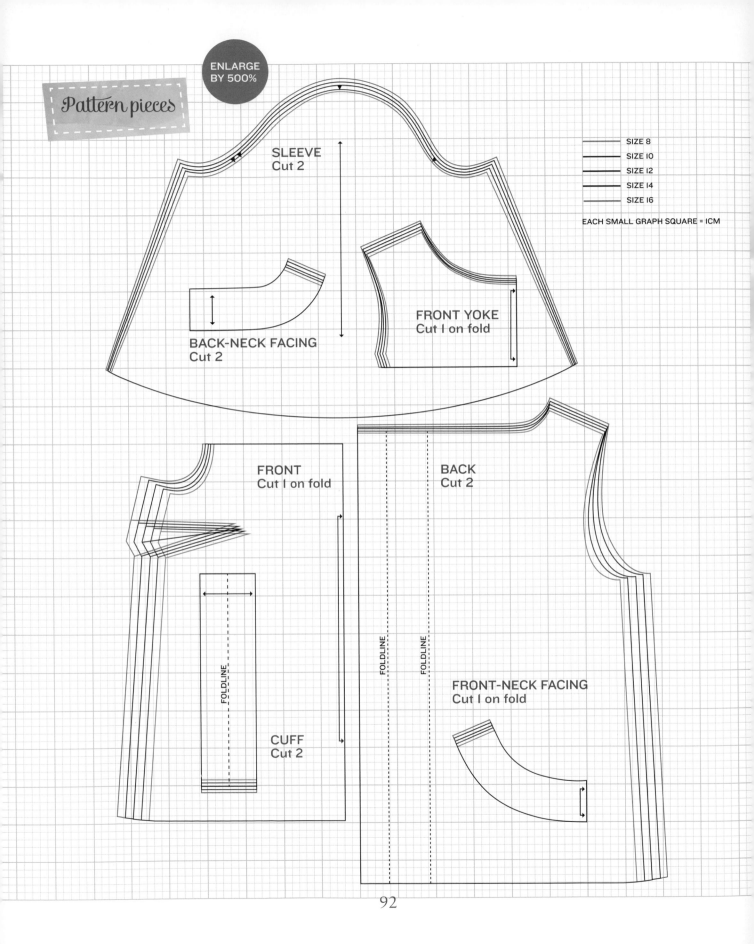

ENLARGE BY 500%

Pattern pieces

SLEEVE
Cut 2

SIZE 8
SIZE 10
SIZE 12
SIZE 14
SIZE 16

EACH SMALL GRAPH SQUARE = 1CM

FRONT YOKE
Cut 1 on fold

BACK-NECK FACING
Cut 2

FRONT
Cut 1 on fold

BACK
Cut 2

FOLDLINE

FOLDLINE

FOLDLINE

FRONT-NECK FACING
Cut 1 on fold

CUFF
Cut 2

Cutting diagram

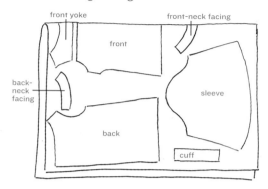

front yoke

front-neck facing

front

back-neck facing

sleeve

back

cuff

Cutting guide

Launder and press the fabric thoroughly before cutting.

FROM THE FABRIC:

✂ Cut one blouse front, one front yoke and one front-neck facing, all on the fold.

✂ Cut two blouse backs, two back-neck facings, two sleeves and two cuffs.

FROM THE IRON-ON INTERFACING:

✂ Cut one front-neck facing on the fold and two back-neck facings.

A 1.5cm (⅝in) seam allowance is included on all the pattern pieces, and a 2cm (¾in) hem allowance on the bottom edges of the blouse front and backs.

To make the blouse

PREPARE THE FRONT

Stitch the two darts on the front and press them downwards. Pin and tack the ready-made piping to the right side of the top of the front, aligning the piping seamline (as close to the piping as possible) with the front seamline. With right sides together, pin and tack the front yoke to the front (on top of the piping), aligning the raw edges of the front and the yoke. Using a zip foot, stitch the three layers together. Remove the tacking. Press the seam downwards so the piping faces upwards. Finish the raw seam edges together, with zigzag or overlocking stitches.

2 STITCH THE BACKS TO THE FRONT

With the right sides of the backs and the front together, stitch the shoulder and side seams. Press the seams open. Finish all raw edges as the seams are stitched. If you prefer, use the French seam method for the exposed seams (see page 56).

3 PREPARE THE NECK FACING

Press the iron-on interfacing onto the wrong sides of the facing pieces. With the right sides together, stitch the front facing to the back facings at the shoulder seams. Press the seams open. Finish all raw edges along the outside edge of the facing only as the shoulder seams will be enclosed under the facing.

4 STITCH ON THE NECK FACING

With right sides together, stitch the facing to the blouse, matching the shoulder seams. The facing does not go all the way to the edge of the back pieces – this is because the centre back edges are folded back in the next step to form button and buttonhole bands. Trim the seam and clip the curves. Press the seams open. Turn the facing to the inside and press along the seam line, pressing the exposed seam allowance at the top of the centre-back edges downwards.

5 STITCH THE BUTTON AND BUTTONHOLE BANDS

Press 4cm (1½in) to the wrong side all along the centre edge of one of the back pieces, pin and tack. Then press 5cm (2in) to the wrong side (this will cover the end of the facing at the neck edge), pin and tack along both sides of the band and along the neck edge. With the wrong side of the blouse facing you, topstitch 3mm (⅛in) from the band folds, starting at the hem edge on one side of the band and stitching up to the neck edge, along the neck edge and back down to the hemline. Remove the tacking and press. Repeat on the other back piece.

6 PREPARE THE SLEEVES
Stitch two lines of gathering stitches across the top of one sleeve, stitching just inside the seam allowance. Do the same across the cuff edge of the sleeve, but stopping and starting the stitching 2cm (¾in) from the side edges. With right sides together, stitch the sleeve seam, taking care not to catch the ends of the gathering threads in the seam. Mark the centre of the top of the sleeve with a pin. Repeat on the other sleeve.

7 STITCH THE SLEEVES TO THE BLOUSE
Turn the blouse wrong side out and one sleeve right side out. Slip the sleeve into the armhole with raw edges aligned. Match the shoulder seam with the sleeve top centre point marked with the pin and align the sleeve seam with the blouse side seam. Pin then tack the lower part of the sleeve into position between the ends of the gathering threads. Draw up the gathering threads so that the sleeve top fits the armhole. Adjust the gathers so they are even and pin, then tack in position. Stitch. Next, work a second line of stitching 6mm (¼in) from the first line. Trim the seam to just outside the second line of stitching and finish the raw edges. Turn the blouse right side out and press the seam towards the sleeve. Repeat with the other sleeve.

8 STITCH ON THE CUFFS
With right sides together, stitch the short edges of one of the cuffs together to form a ring. Press the seam open. Draw up the gathering threads at the bottom of one of the sleeves until it matches the circumference of the cuff. With right sides together, pin the cuff to the gathered sleeve, adjusting the gathers so they are even and fit the cuff. Tack and stitch. Press 1.5cm (⅝in) to the wrong side along the raw edge of the cuff, then fold this edge to the inside of the sleeve, making sure the inside of the cuff overlaps the stitching line. Slipstitch in place. Repeat with the other cuff.

9 HEM THE BLOUSE
Press 1cm (⅜in) to the wrong side twice along the hemline edge of the blouse to form a double hem. Pin and tack. Stitch close to the first fold.

10 MAKE THE BUTTONS AND BUTTONHOLES
Cover the button moulds if you are making fabric-covered buttons. Mark the positions of the vertical buttonholes in the centre of the right back band – the top of the first buttonhole should be 6mm (¼in) below the neck edge and the bottom of last buttonhole 15cm (6in) above the hemline. Machine stitch the buttonholes and sew on the buttons.

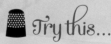

Try this...
If you're using really floppy fabric, you may want to add iron-on interfacing to the button and buttonhole bands. Cut two strips of interfacing 4cm (1½in) wide and as long as the centre back edge. After pressing the folds for the back bands and before stitching the bands, open out and press on the interfacing between the folds.

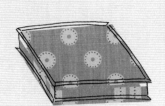

FLOOR CUSHION

*Box cushions are surprisingly easy to make, especially
if you topstitch the edges for a smart finish. Once
you've mastered the art of making them, you'll be able
to re-cover sofa and chair cushions, or make generous
garden or window seat cushions.*

DIFFICULTY RATING: ●● ●● ●● ●● ●●

Materials

1.6m (1¾yd) of a medium-
   to heavy-weight
   furnishing fabric print at
   least 115cm (45in) wide,
   for main fabric
60cm (¾yd) of the same
   weight furnishing fabric
   in a contrasting print,
   for sides
70cm (27¾in) nylon zip,
   to match main fabric
Matching sewing thread
Cushion pad to fit finished
   cover

A generously proportioned box cushion works well on the floor
and is so much more tailored than a beanbag or pouffe. Made
in a neutral tone, it will team with almost any interior scheme.
Made supersize like this for the floor, you can use them to
provide extra coffee-table height seating when all other chairs are
occupied, or even allocate one as a sitting-room smart dog bed.

CUSHION SIZE
The finished floor cushion measures 70 x 70 x 10cm
(27¾ x 27¾ x 4in).

FABRIC FINDER
Floor cushions take a lot of wear and tear and should be covered
in a furnishing fabric suitable for upholstery, which will be durable
and meet all the necessary fire regulations. Being a floor cushion,
machine washable is best – check the care label and wash to pre-
shrink before making up.
Try these alternatives:
**Heavy-duty pure linen—Heavy-duty pure cotton—Linen union—
Cotton duck—Canvas—Ticking**

SKILLS SET
Stitching straight seams see page 51—Finishing seams see pages 54 and 55
Inserting a centred zip see pages 64 and 65—Topstitching edges to imitate piping see step 5 on page 99

Cutting guide

Press the fabric thoroughly before cutting. Measure and mark the fabric using a steel rule and ensure all the corners are at perfect right angles before cutting.

FROM THE MAIN FABRIC:

✂ Cut one piece for the top, measuring 73 x 73cm (29 x 29in).

✂ Cut two pieces for the bottom, one measuring 73 x 58cm (29 x 22¾in) and the other 73 x 18cm (29 x 7¼in).

FROM THE CONTRASTING FABRIC:

✂ Cut four pieces for the sides, each measuring 73 x 13cm (29 x 5¼in).

To make the floor cushion

1 INSERT THE ZIP

As linen frays readily, finish all the edges first. Next, fold under and press a 1.5cm (⅝in) seam allowance along one long edge of each bottom piece. Open out the folds and with right sides together tack along the fold – this is the seam the zip goes in. Stitch together 1.5cm (⅝in) at each end of the seam, leaving the centre 70cm (27¾in) open for the zip. Lay the joined bottom face down and place the closed zip face down on top, centred on the seam. Tack and stitch the centred zip in place. Remove all the tacking, then press the zip opening from the front.

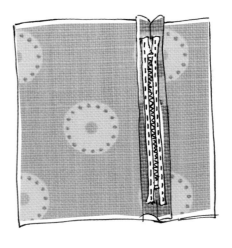

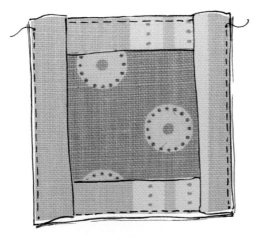

2 STITCH THE SIDES TO THE TOP

With right sides together, pin a contrasting side piece to one edge of the top piece. Starting 1.5cm (⅝in) in from one corner, stitch the seam leaving a 1.5cm (⅝in) seam allowance and stopping 1.5cm (⅝in) before you reach the end of the seam. Sew on the remaining three sides in the same way. Press the seams open.

3 STITCH THE SIDES TO THE BOTTOM
Stitch the bottom of the cushion cover to the sides, stitching each seam in the same direction and sequence as you did for the top. Press the seams open.

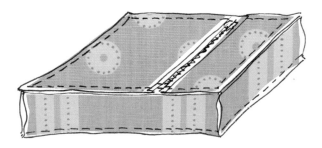

4 STITCH THE CORNERS
Stitch the corner seams, stopping at the seamline for nice crisp corners. Press these short corner seams open. Next, press all the long seams flat towards the contrasting sides.

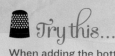 Try this...

When adding the bottom, always stitch following the same sequence and in the same direction as for the front. This is so that the cushion cover will lie square. If you stitch in the opposite direction, you may get a cross pull.

5 TOPSTITCH THE EDGES
Unzip and turn the cover right side out. Then fold exactly along each seamline to sandwich the seam allowance between the layers, and press. This will make the topstitching easier. Topstitch along all the seams 3mm (⅛in) from the edge for an instant faux piping effect. Insert the cushion pad and close the zip.

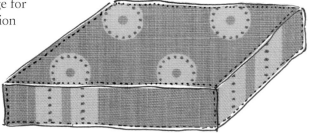

EDGE-TO-EDGE JACKET

Cut short and simple, this jacket is more casual than a work jacket but smarter than a cardigan. Make it in either wool or linen and wear it over dresses, skirts or jeans.

DIFFICULTY RATING:

Many classic jackets are frankly difficult to make, especially when they involve linings, tricky collars, set-in sleeves and pockets – it is where dressmaking borders on tailoring. But here's a jacket that is easy to sew. It's collarless, edge-to-edge and lining-free, so dodges all the difficult tasks whilst offering the basic elements of jacket construction.

JACKET SIZES
To fit UK women's sizes 8, 10, 12, 14 and 16.

FABRIC FINDER
Lightweight wool is an excellent mid-season choice that would get you through spring and autumn. It also resists creasing and drapes well for a stay-smart look.
Try these alternatives:
Bouclé wool weave—Wool tweed—Wool twill—Wool blends—Linen and linen blends

Materials
1.8m (2yd) of wool fabric 140cm (55in) wide
80 x 50cm (32 x 20in) of lightweight iron-on interfacing
1.5m (1¾yd) satin ribbon 1cm (⅜in) wide
6 buttons 2.5cm (1in) in diameter
Sewing thread to match main fabric
Sewing thread to match ribbon

SKILLS SET
Working even slipstitch see page 48
Stitching straight seams see page 51—Clipping curved seams see page 52
Finishing seams see pages 54 and 55—Easing see page 63

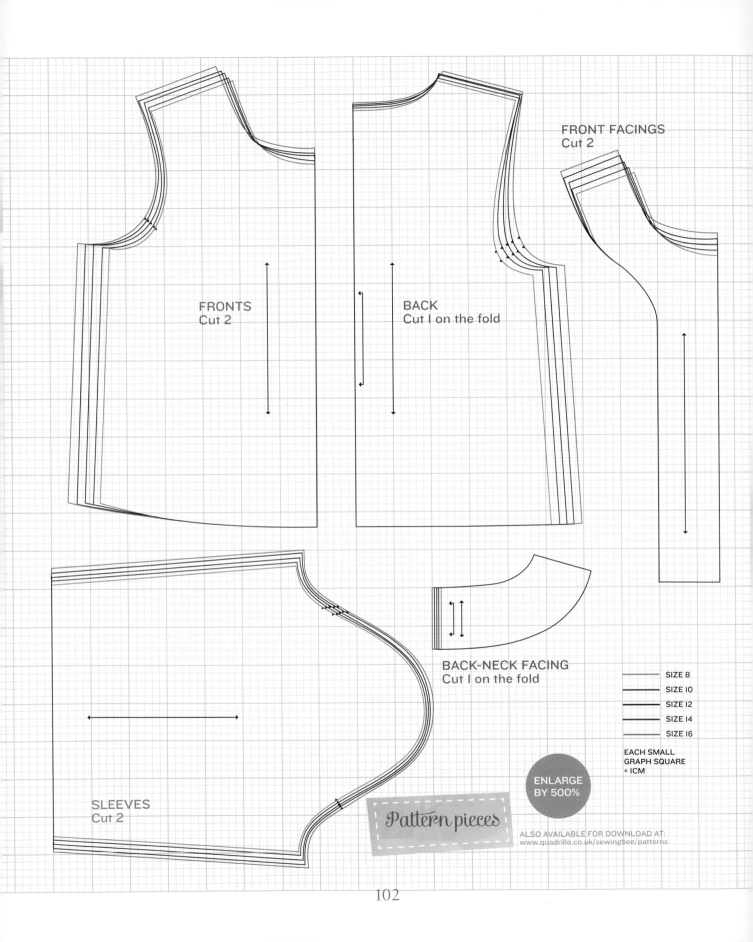

FRONT FACINGS
Cut 2

FRONTS
Cut 2

BACK
Cut I on the fold

BACK-NECK FACING
Cut I on the fold

SLEEVES
Cut 2

SIZE 8
SIZE 10
SIZE 12
SIZE 14
SIZE 16

EACH SMALL
GRAPH SQUARE
= ICM

ENLARGE
BY 500%

Pattern pieces

ALSO AVAILABLE FOR DOWNLOAD AT:
www.quadrille.co.uk/sewingbee/patterns

Cutting diagram

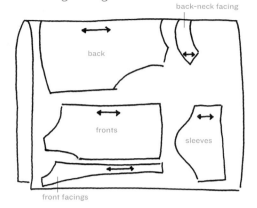

back-neck facing

back

fronts

sleeves

front facings

Cutting guide

Press the fabric thoroughly before cutting.

FROM THE FABRIC:

✄ Cut two jacket fronts, two front facings and two sleeves.

✄ Cut one jacket back and one back-neck facing, both on the fold.

A 1.5cm (⅝in) seam allowance is included on all the pattern pieces, and a 5.5cm (2¼in) hem allowance on the bottom edges of the fronts, back and sleeves. Note: the front facings are shorter than the jacket front pieces.

To make the jacket

1 STITCH THE BACK AND FRONTS TOGETHER
Machine stitch a line of stay stitching around the neckline on both fronts and the back. With right sides together, stitch the shoulder seams and the side seams. Finish the raw seam edges and press the seams open. Turn up and stitch a 1cm (⅜in) hem all along the bottom edge of the jacket.

2 PREPARE THE FACING
Cut out and press the iron-on interfacing onto the wrong sides of the front facings and back-neck facing. With right sides together, stitch the shoulder seams of the prepared facing pieces. Press the seams open. Turn in and stitch a 1cm (⅜in) hem to the wrong side along the inside edge of the prepared facing.

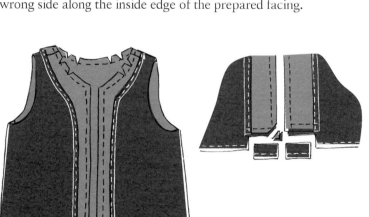

3 STITCH ON THE FACING
Pin the facing to the jacket with right sides together, matching the shoulder seams, then the back neckline between these, each front edge and finally pin along each short end of the facing. Tack and then stitch. Trim the seams and cut off the jacket hems below the facing to align with the bottom of the facing as shown, but be sure to leave an overlap on the jacket hem that will be hidden behind the facing. Snip off the corners of the seam allowances at the hem edge. Clip the curved seams around the neckline.

4 TACK THE HEM IN PLACE
Turn the facing to the inside of the jacket, turning up the hemline by 4.5cm (1¾in) to lie behind the end of the facing. Pin and tack the entire hem into position.

5 ADD THE RIBBON TRIM
Starting at the facing on the inside of the jacket (see step 4) and over to the front of the jacket, pin and tack the ribbon in position at the top of the hemline about 2.5cm (1in) from the hemline fold, and continue the ribbon all along the hem and over onto the other facing. Topstitch the ribbon in place, stitching close to each edge. On the inside of the jacket, slipstitch the end of the facing to the jacket hem.

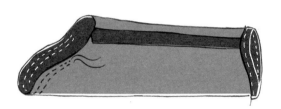

6 PREPARE THE SLEEVES
At the top of the sleeves, work two lines of easing stitches. With right sides together, stitch the sleeve seams. Finish the raw seam edges and press the seams open. Turn up 1cm (⅜in) around the bottom edges of the sleeves and stitch.

7 STITCH ON THE SLEEVES
Turn the sleeves right side out and the jacket wrong side out. Pin the right sides of one sleeve and one armhole together, matching the dots. Tack from the side seam up to the lower dot on one side. Return to the side seam and tack up to the other dot. Pull up the easing threads until the sleeve fits the armhole. Distribute the gathers evenly and tack the sleeve into position. Stitch. Repeat with the other sleeve. Clip the underarm curved seams.

8 FINISH THE SLEEVE HEMS
Turn up the sleeve hem as for the jacket fronts and back and tack it in place. Now add the ribbon trim. Measure 2.5cm (1in) from the hem fold at several points around the sleeve and pin the ribbon in position. Tack, then topstitch close to each edge.

9 STITCH ON THE BUTTONS
Stitch three buttons to each front, 3cm (1¼in) from the front edge – position the top button about 11cm (4¼in) below the neck edge and the other two 4.5cm (1¾in) apart below the first.

PENCIL SKIRT

Easy to sew, skirts are an excellent first garment project. Admittedly, some sewers find zips a little tricky, but take your time and tack at every stage. A pencil skirt like this one is a useful classic pattern.

DIFFICULTY RATING:

Learn to make this basic skirt, and you'll have all the skills to make almost any skirt you want. The key elements are stitching darts, inserting zips and putting on waistbands. Use exactly the same methods to make easy-to-wear A-lines, a shorter mini or even something long.

PENCIL SKIRT SIZES

To fit UK women's sizes 8, 10, 12, 14 and 16.

FABRIC FINDER

A pencil skirt can be made from any fabric you like. But if you are making one for the first time, choose a fabric that will be easy to stitch – a cotton fabric that is neither too thick nor too thin. If it is for the office, stick to sophisticated prints in dark tones. The herringbone weave of this mixed-fibre fabric is smart enough to take you anywhere, whilst giving the skirt a flattering drape.

Try these alternatives:

Laundered cotton—Denim—Challis—Lightweight wool and wool blends—Jacquard—Linen and linen blends—Gabardine—Lightweight twill

SKILLS SET

Working even slipstitch **see page 48**—Slipstitching double-fold hems **see page 50**
Stitching straight seams **see page 51**—Finishing seams **see pages 54 and 55**
Stitching single-point darts **see page 60**—Inserting an invisible zip **see pages 68 and 69**

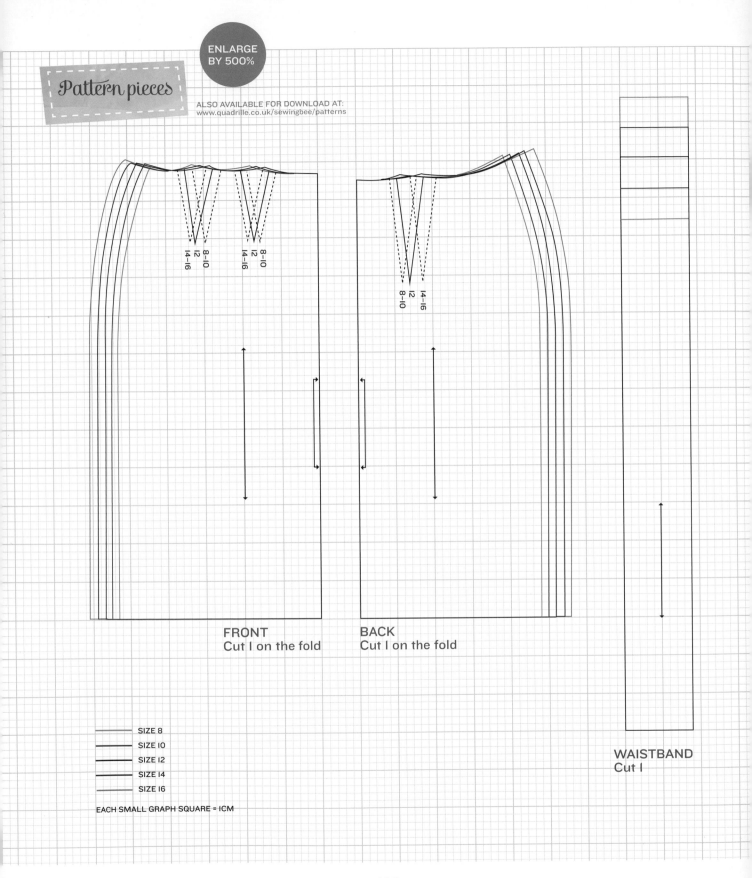

ENLARGE
BY 500%

Pattern pieces

ALSO AVAILABLE FOR DOWNLOAD AT:
www.quadrille.co.uk/sewingbee/patterns

8–10
12
14–16

8–10
12
14–16

8–10
12
14–16

FRONT
Cut 1 on the fold

BACK
Cut 1 on the fold

WAISTBAND
Cut 1

SIZE 8
SIZE 10
SIZE 12
SIZE 14
SIZE 16

EACH SMALL GRAPH SQUARE = 1CM

108

Cutting diagram

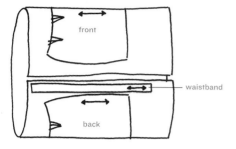

Cutting guide

Press the fabric thoroughly before cutting.

FROM THE FABRIC:

✂ Cut one skirt front and one skirt back, both on the fold.

✂ Cut one waistband.

A 1.5cm (⅝in) seam allowance is included on all the pattern pieces, and a 2.5cm (1in) hem allowance on the bottom edges of the skirt front and back.

To make the pencil skirt

1 STITCH THE DARTS
Stitch the four darts on the skirt front and the two darts on the skirt back and then press them towards the centre.

2 STITCH THE SIDE SEAMS AND INSERT THE ZIP
With right sides together, pin the skirt front to the skirt back along the side seams. Using a 1.5cm (⅝in) seam allowance, insert the invisible zip in the left side-seam of the skirt, and complete the seam from the bottom of the zip to the hem. (When the wrong side of the front of the skirt is facing you, the zip opening is on the left of the front piece.) Next, stitch the right side seam all the way from the waist edge to the hem edge. Press the seams open and finish the raw seam edges.

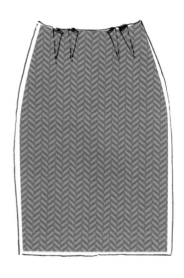

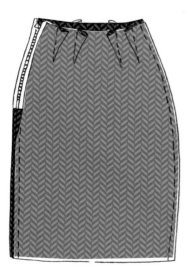

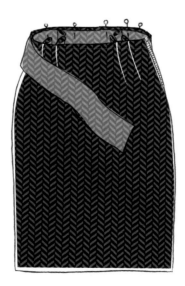

3 STITCH THE WAISTBAND TO THE SKIRT
Turn the skirt right side out. Fold the waistband in half lengthways and mark the centre point with a pin. With right sides together, pin the waistband to the skirt. Start by matching the marker pin with the right side seam then work around the waistband until you reach the zip. Stitch 1.5cm (⅝in) from the raw edges. Trim the seam.

4 PRESS THE WAISTBAND SEAM
Press open the waistband seam, then press the waistband and all the fabric within the seams upwards.

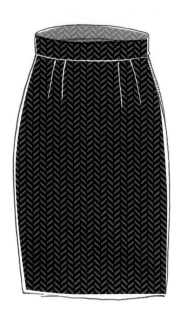

5 COMPLETE THE WAISTBAND
Press under 1.5cm (⅝in) along the free raw edge of the waistband. Pin this edge to the back of the waistband so it covers the line of stitching just completed. Tuck the raw short edges to the inside of the waistband so they enclose the ends of the zip tape. Tack then topstitch the waistband in place along the waistband seam. Slipstitch the short edges of the waistband together to finish. Press the completed waistband. Stitch the hooks onto one end of the waistband and the eyes to the other.

6 HEM THE SKIRT
For a quick, neat hem, machine stitch it neatly in place. To do this, turn up 12mm (½in) twice along the hem, press and tack. Machine stitch this double hem, stitching close to the first fold.

Try this...

To give your waistband some added stiffness, press iron-on interfacing onto the front half of the band. And when topstitching the finished waistband, topstitch both the top and bottom edges.
MAY MARTIN

SUMMER DRESS

This empire-line dress flatters every figure and its versatility means it can be dressed up with heels or down with sandals. However, as it's made from six main pieces, a midriff band and pockets, this is a project for more experienced sewers.

DIFFICULTY RATING: ⦿ ⦿ ⦿ ⦿ ⦂

Materials

- 2.8m (3yd) of a medium-weight cotton print, at least 115cm (45in) wide, for main fabric
- 90cm (1yd) of a lightweight cotton fabric, at least 112cm- (44in-) wide, for bodice lining
- 15 x 60cm (6 x 24in) of lightweight iron-on interfacing, for midriff front
- Matching zip, 35cm (14in) long
- Matching sewing thread

F abrics are the Unique Selling Point of making-your-own clothes. Unless you have an unlimited budget, off-the-peg clothes are by necessity sold in limited colours to appeal to a wide market. Yet a single dress shape can look very different depending on fabric choice so this is where you can really express your own style. This dress, made by one of *The Great British Sewing Bee* contestants from a pattern by Simplicity, is admittedly not the simplest to make with its shaped bodice, pleated skirt and pockets. But it's well worth the effort. Cut flatteringly to fit only around the neckline and midriff band, the pleated skirt skims obligingly over the hips and falls to an elegant straight hem.

SUMMER DRESS SIZES
To fit UK women's sizes 8, 10, 12, 14 and 16.

FABRIC FINDER
The structure of this dress demands a fabric with plenty of body for a flattering fit and to emphasise its elegant shape.
Try these alternatives:
Densely woven cotton and cotton blends—Lightweight denim—Chambray—Lightweight wool and wool blends—Jacquard—Shantung—Taffeta

SKILLS SET
Working even slipstitch **see page 48**—Slipstitching double-fold hems **see page 50**
Stitching straight seams **see page 51**—Clipping curved seams **see page 52**
Finishing seams **see pages 54 and 55**—Inserting a lapped zip **see pages 66 and 67**

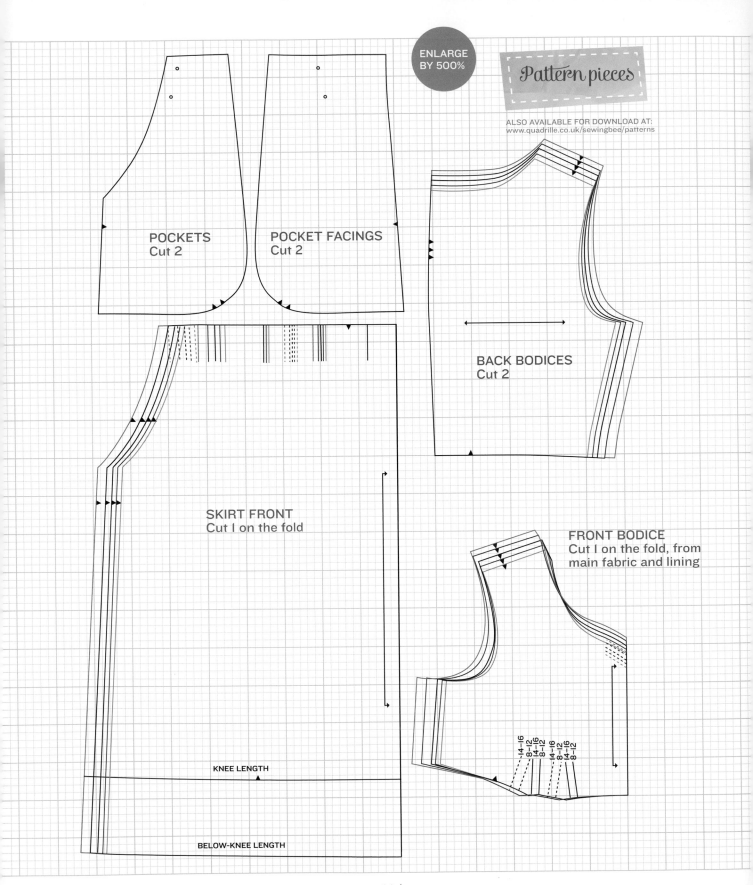

ENLARGE
BY 500%

Pattern pieces

ALSO AVAILABLE FOR DOWNLOAD AT:
www.quadrille.co.uk/sewingbee/patterns

POCKETS
Cut 2

POCKET FACINGS
Cut 2

BACK BODICES
Cut 2

SKIRT FRONT
Cut I on the fold

FRONT BODICE
Cut I on the fold, from
main fabric and lining

14–16
8–12
14–16
8–12
14–16
8–12
14–16
8–12

KNEE LENGTH

BELOW-KNEE LENGTH

SIZE 8
SIZE 10
SIZE 12
SIZE 14
SIZE 16

EACH SMALL GRAPH SQUARE = 1CM

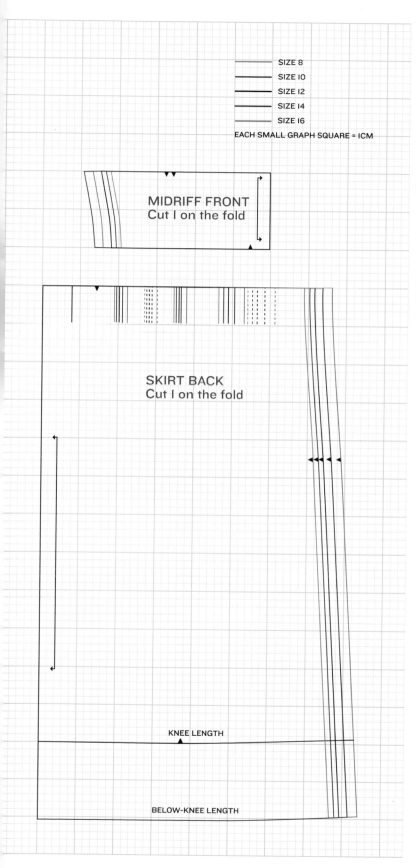

MIDRIFF FRONT
Cut 1 on the fold

SKIRT BACK
Cut 1 on the fold

KNEE LENGTH

BELOW-KNEE LENGTH

Cutting diagrams

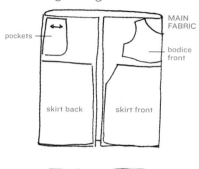

pockets

MAIN FABRIC

bodice front

skirt back   skirt front

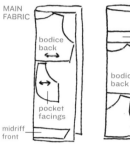

MAIN FABRIC

bodice back

midriff front

pocket facings

midriff front

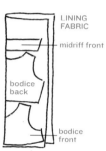

LINING FABRIC

midriff front

bodice back

bodice front

Cutting guide

Press the fabric thoroughly before cutting.

FROM THE MAIN FABRIC AND THE LINING:

✄ Cut two bodice backs.

✄ Cut one bodice front and one midriff front, both on the fold.

FROM THE MAIN FABRIC:

✄ Cut one skirt front and one skirt back, both on the fold.

✄ Cut two pockets and two pocket facings.

FROM THE INTERFACING:

✄ Cut one midriff front.

A 1.5cm (⅝in) seam allowance is included on all the pattern pieces, and a 2.5cm (1in) hem allowance on the bottom edges of the skirt front and back. Choose either the longer or shorter length when cutting the skirt pieces.

Try this...

You can simplify the design of this dress considerably by omitting the pockets. Adapt the pattern by continuing the line of the front skirt piece to match the shape of the back skirt.

To make the summer dress

1 PREPARE THE BODICE
With right sides together, place the bodice backs to the bodice front at the shoulder seams. Stitch, taking a 1.5cm (⅝in) seam allowance throughout. Press the shoulder seams open. Repeat with the front and back bodice lining.

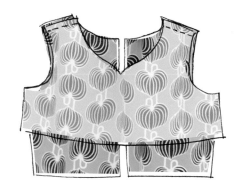

2 STITCH THE BODICE TO THE BODICE LINING
With right sides together, pin the bodice lining to the bodice, matching the shoulder seams and the point of the V-neck. Stitch all along the neck edge and around the armholes. Reinforce the V by re-stitching over the original line of stitching. Trim the seams, clip the curved seams and clip into the V, all the time being careful not to cut the stitching. Turn the lining to the inside by pulling each back through the front at the shoulder seam. Press.

3 STITCH THE BODICE CENTRE BACK SEAM
Open up the whole piece so that you can place the centre back edges right sides together. Pin the seam from the bottom of the lining, up, through the seam joining the lining to the bodice at the neck, and then down to the hem of the main bodice piece. Stitch and press the seam open. Turn the lining to the inside and press. Tack the raw edges of the two layers of the bodice front together along the side and bottom edges.

4 PLEAT THE BODICE FRONT
Fold along one solid line at the lower edge of the bodice front and bring the fold to the broken line. Pin. Repeat for the other folds. Tack all along the raw edge through the pleats.

5 STITCH ON THE MIDRIFF FRONT

Start by ironing the interfacing onto the wrong side of the midriff-front piece. With right sides together and raw edges aligned, pin the upper edge of the interfaced midriff front to the lower edge of the bodice front, then pin the midriff-lining to the other side in the same way. Tack through all layers and stitch. Press the midriff front and lining downwards, and tack them together along the side and bottom edges.

6 STITCH THE BODICE'S RIGHT SIDE SEAM

With the bodice wrong side out, open out the right side-seam edge of the back bodice and wrap it over the right side-seam edge on the front bodice, with the right sides of the front and back lining together and the right sides of the front and back bodice together and the raw edges aligned. Pin and stitch the right side seam through all four layers.

7 STITCH THE POCKET FACINGS TO THE SKIRT FRONT

With right sides together, pin the pocket facing to the skirt front. Stitch along the curved skirt edge. Trim the seam and clip the curves. Turn the facing to the inside and press. Repeat with the other pocket.

8 STITCH ON THE POCKETS

On the inside of the skirt front, with right sides together and raw edges aligned, pin the pocket piece to the pocket facing. Stitch the curved outer edge, leaving the side seam and top edges unstitched. Repeat with the other pocket.

9 TACK THE POCKET IN PLACE

Align the top and the side seam raw edges of the pocket and its facing with the skirt front and tack the pockets securely in place along these edges.

10 PREPARE THE SKIRT

With right sides together, stitch the skirt back to the skirt front. On the left seam, stitch from the lower edge to the notch (where the zip starts), then work a few extra reverse stitches for strength. On the right seam, stitch from the hem to the top. Press the seams open.

11 PLEAT THE SKIRT

Start with one centre front pleat by folding along the solid line and folding it to the centre front. Pin, placing the pins vertically at the folds. Repeat with the other centre front pleat. For the remaining front pleats, fold along the solid lines and bring to the broken lines, pinning as you go. Repeat the whole process on the back of the skirt. Tack across the front and back upper edges of the skirt.

12 STITCH THE SKIRT TO THE BODICE

With right sides together, pin the skirt to the bodice, matching the right side seams and left opening edges. Tack and stitch. Press the seam up towards the bodice and finish the raw seam edges with machine zigzag or overlocking stitches.

13 INSERT THE ZIP

Insert the zip using the lapped method, aligning the top of the teeth with the armhole. Turn the top of the zip tapes under and slipstitch to neaten.

14 STITCH THE HEM

Machine stitch or slipstitch a double hem along the lower edge of the skirt.

LAUNDRY BAG

Making a channel for a drawstring is the key skill you'll learn when stitching this bag. It's a really useful technique that you'll be able to put to use in so many ways – from bags to garments, such as pyjama trousers and drawstring skirts.

DIFFICULTY RATING:

Materials
1.9m (2¼yd) of 115cm-
(45in-) wide fabric
10cm (4in) of grosgrain
ribbon, 4cm (1½in) wide
Sewing threads to match
fabric and ribbon

Drawstring bags are easy to make and stitching them is a great skill to learn. This one's been made with a gusset to give it a three-dimensional quality for extra room, but you can use the same principles for bags of all sizes and shapes. Adapt the bag to make kids' shoe bags, ballet, gym and other kit bags, by cutting the main pieces smaller and simplify by using just a front and back piece.

LAUNDRY BAG SIZE
The finished bag measures 48cm (19in) wide x 74cm (29in) tall x 11cm (4¼in) deep.

FABRIC FINDER
This embroidered brushed gingham is a great choice for a laundry bag as it's robust yet pretty.
Try these alternatives:
Classic gingham—Cotton duck—Denim—Chambray—Gabardine—
Ticking—Brushed cotton—Seersucker

SKILLS SET
Stitching straight seams **see page 51**

Cutting guide

Press the fabric thoroughly before cutting. Determine how you're going to cut the pieces from the fabric, so you leave room to cut the long drawstring strips along the length of the fabric.

FROM THE FABRIC:

✁ Cut one piece for the bag front panel and one for the back panel, each 50 x 93cm (20 x 37in)

✁ Cut two pieces for the side panels, each 13 x 93cm (5¼ x 37in)

✁ Cut one piece for the bag base, measuring 13 x 50cm (5¼ x 20in)

✁ Cut two strips for the drawstrings, each 5 x 175cm (2 x 69in)

✁ Cut one strip for the hanging loop, measuring 5 x 36cm (2 x 14in)

To make the laundry bag

1 MAKE THE DRAWSTRINGS AND THE HANGING LOOP

Fold one of the long drawstring strips in half lengthways with the wrong sides together and press. Open out the strip, fold 12mm (½in) toward the centre along each long edge and press. Refold the strip along the centre and press again for a 12mm (½in) drawstring width. Clip each end on the diagonal and topstitch all along the long edge of the drawstring, stitching close to the edge. Repeat for the other drawstring and the hanging loop, but don't cut a diagonal end on the hanging loop.

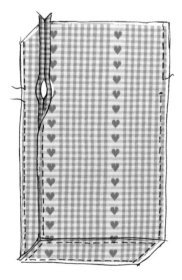

2 STITCH THE BAG PIECES TOGETHER

With right sides together, pin the long edge of the front panel to the long edge of one side panel. Mark a seam opening from 60cm to 65cm (23½in to 25½in) from the bottom edge (this is the position of the drawstring channel). Starting 1cm (⅜in) from the bottom edge and leaving a 1cm (⅜in) seam allowance, stitch the panels together all the way to the top edge. Remember to leave 5cm (2in) open in the seam where marked and make a few extra reverse stitches either side of the opening for strength. Stitch the other side panel to the front in exactly the same way, leaving the opening for the drawstring channel. Stitch the back panel to the side panels in the same way. You now have a rectangular tube. Stitch on the base panel, leaving a 1cm (⅜in) seam allowance. Press all seams open, and press the seam allowances along the drawstring-channel openings to the wrong side.

3 MAKE THE DRAWSTRING CHANNEL

Turn 1cm (⅜in) to the wrong side around the top of the laundry bag, press and pin. Topstitch this hem. Next, fold 17cm (7in) of the top of the bag to the wrong side. Press the fold at the top and tack this turning in place along the fold and along the hem. Stitch all around the bag 10cm (4in) from the upper folded edge – take the sewing bed off your machine if it detaches. Work another line of stitching 5cm (2in) below this – make sure these two stitching lines are aligned with the top and bottom of the prepared slit openings for the drawstrings.

4 INSERT THE DRAWSTRING

Starting at the left opening, use a large safety pin to thread one drawstring through the channel on the front, over the outside of the bag at the side panel, then through the channel on the back, so ending up on the other side of the side panel from where you started. Repeat with the other drawstring, this time, starting at the right opening. Knot the ends of the drawstrings.

5 STITCH ON THE HANGING LOOP

Fold the hanging loop in half and pin the ends side by side to the centre back, with the raw edges about 7.5cm (3in) from the top of the bag – approximately 2.5cm (1in) above the upper stitching line of the drawstring channel. Cut a 8cm (3in) length of 4cm- (1½in-) wide ribbon, fold in the raw edges to form a 4cm (1½in) square, and pin in place over the ends of the hanging loop. Stitch all around the grosgrain square, close the edge, then stitch an 'X' from corner to corner for extra strength.

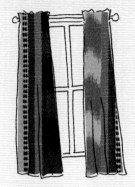

BASIC CURTAINS

If you can sew a straight line then you can make a pair of curtains. They're really not difficult to make, especially if you stitch purpose-made gathering tape at the top for fool-proof perfect pleats.

DIFFICULTY RATING: ⊞ ⊞ ⊞ ⊞ ⊞

The key to sewing perfect curtains is careful measuring at every step to ensure all the angles are square and hemlines straight. You need a large flat surface to work on, and while the professionals might have generously proportioned benches to work on, a clean floor is as good a place as any to lay out the fabric before carefully cutting it to size.

CURTAIN SIZE
The basic curtain can be made to fit any window size.

FABRIC FINDER
These curtains are made in a heavy-weight 100 per cent cotton, which is easy to handle and always looks smart. Although curtains can be made from almost any fabric, you'll get best results from curtain or upholstery fabrics, which generally cut out the light and come in wider-than-fashion-fabric widths.
Try these alternatives:
Heavy-weight linens—Linen union—Curtain-weight silk—Chintz—Jacquard—Dupion

Materials
Curtain fabric in the
   required amount
Curtain lining fabric in
   the required amount
Curtain heading tape,
   for gathering the
   curtain top
Hooks to fit the curtain
   tape
Matching sewing thread
2 metal curtain-weight
   rings for each curtain

SKILLS SET
Stitching straight seams see page 51
Working even and uneven slipstitch see pages 48 and 49

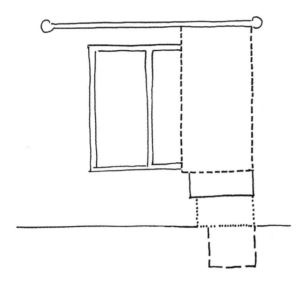

Measuring guide

FOR THE FINISHED CURTAIN LENGTH:
Measure from the top of the curtain rail to the floor, or to
the bottom edge of the windowsill if you want short curtains.
The length is know as the curtain 'drop'.
FOR THE FINISHED CURTAIN WIDTH:
Measure the curtain rail and double this figure. (If you are making
a pair of curtains for the rail, then each finished curtain width
should be half this amount.)

Cutting guide

FROM THE CURTAIN FABRIC:
✂ Cut a panel of fabric that is as long as
the desired curtain 'drop' plus 25cm (10in)
extra – this extra amount allows 20cm (8in)
for a double hem at the bottom and a 5cm
(2in) turn-down at the top. The width of
the panel should be twice the length of the
curtain rail, plus 13cm (5¼in) extra – this
allows for a 6.5cm (2⅝in) turn-back along
each side of the curtain. You might have to
stitch together two or more drops to achieve
the width you need. If in doubt, show the
window dimensions to the retailer and they
will help you to work out what you need.
FROM THE LINING FABRIC:
✂ Cut a panel of fabric that is 5cm (2in)
shorter than the curtain fabric and 10cm
(4in) narrower.

To make the curtain

1 CUT OUT THE CURTAIN AND LINING PANELS
Determine the size of your finished curtain as explained in
the Measuring Guide, then cut out the curtain and lining panels
as explained in the Cutting Guide.

**2 HEM THE CURTAIN
AND LINING**
Press up a 10cm (4in) hem
along the bottom raw edges of
the curtain and lining fabrics,
then turn up by another 10cm
(4in) and stitch the bottom
hem in place on both pieces.
Use uneven slipstitch on the
curtain fabric and a regular
straight machine stitch for the
lining hem. Press the hems
from the wrong side.

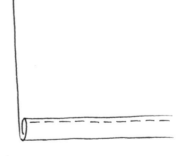

3 STITCH THE LINING TO THE CURTAIN

Now stitch the lining to the curtain along the side edges. With right sides together, position the lining hem 5cm (2in) higher than the main curtain, measuring several times along its length to ensure it is straight and ensuring the sides are at perfect right angles to the hem. Pin, then machine stitch the side seams together, taking 1.5cm (⅝in) seam allowances. Press the seams towards the lining and turn right side out.

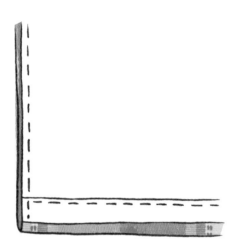

4 FINISH THE HEM CORNERS

Lay the curtain right side down on a flat surface, making sure the lining is centred on the main fabric – there is 5cm (2in) more of the curtain fabric at each side edge of the lining. Smooth out any creases. Press. At the hem corners, fold in the raw edge of the curtain fabric at a 45-degree angle to hide it. Slipstitch the diagonal fold in place, using the even slipstitch technique.

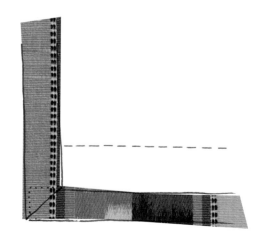

5 ADD THE HEADING TAPE

Starting at the hemline, measure the desired length of the curtain (the calculated drop) up to the top. Do this several times across the width of the curtain, marking the length at the top with tailor's chalk, then use a steel rule to mark the top position along the width of the curtain – it will be about 5cm (2in) below the raw edges at the top, but this is your chance to slightly adjust the length. Turn both layers to the wrong side along this line and pin, placing the pins at right angles to the curtain top. Place the heading tape along the width of the curtain, close to the top edge and covering the raw edges. Fold in each end of the tape by 3cm (1¼in), making sure the hook pockets are right side up and the cords are free from where you will be stitching. Pin the gathering tape in position, folding the curtain turn-down under the tape at each end of the tape. Stitch the tape in place along the top edge first; then go back to the first short side and stitch along it, along the lower edge and finally the last short side.

6 COMPLETE THE FINISHING TOUCHES

Lastly, draw up the strings from both ends of the tape, evenly distributing the gathers to your required width, and secure with a knot or use cord tidies (easier for dry cleaning). Put in your curtain hooks and hang the curtain. At the hem, tuck a curtain-weight ring inside the hem at each corner at the bottom of the curtain and stitch it in place.

Try this...
Curtain fabric can be quite thick, so be sure to match your sewing machine needle to the weight of your fabric – a needle that is too fine could snap off during stitching. MAY MARTIN

CIRCULAR SKIRT

Cut as two half circles – or sometimes as one complete circle – circular skirts are simple to make. The inside circle is stitched flat into the waistband, then the folds flow smoothly over the hips, offering fullness at the hem.

DIFFICULTY RATING: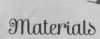

With no darts or gathers to deal with, circular skirts are about the easiest to make. Yet once you've learned the technique, they're surprisingly versatile, taking on a completely different personality depending on the length. Cut it long for floor-sweeping evening elegance, or if you love your legs go thigh high for cheer-leader chirpiness.

SKIRT SIZES
To fit UK women's sizes 8, 10, 12, 14 and 16.
The finished length is approximately 58cm (22½in), but the length is easily adjustable.

FABRIC FINDER
Circular skirts can be made from almost any fabric, but aim for one that has body and graceful fluidity. Floor length skirts will need less body as they become very wide at the hem.
Try these alternatives for daywear:
Laundered cotton—Lightweight denim—Chambray—Challis—
Seersucker—Silk linen—Cotton jersey
Try these alternatives for eveningwear:
Fine silk—Fine satin—Taffeta—Silk/polyester mixes

Materials
3m (3¼yd) of a fine, tightly
   woven linen print at
   least 115cm (45in) wide
Matching invisible zip,
   23cm (9in) long
Two 1–1.5cm (³⁄₈–½in)
   buttons
Matching sewing thread

SKILLS SET
Slipstitching double-fold hems **see page 50**— Stitching straight seams **see page 51**
Finishing seams **see pages 54 and 55**— Inserting an invisible zip **see pages 68 and 69**
Making buttonholes **see page 72**— Adding buttons **see page 73**

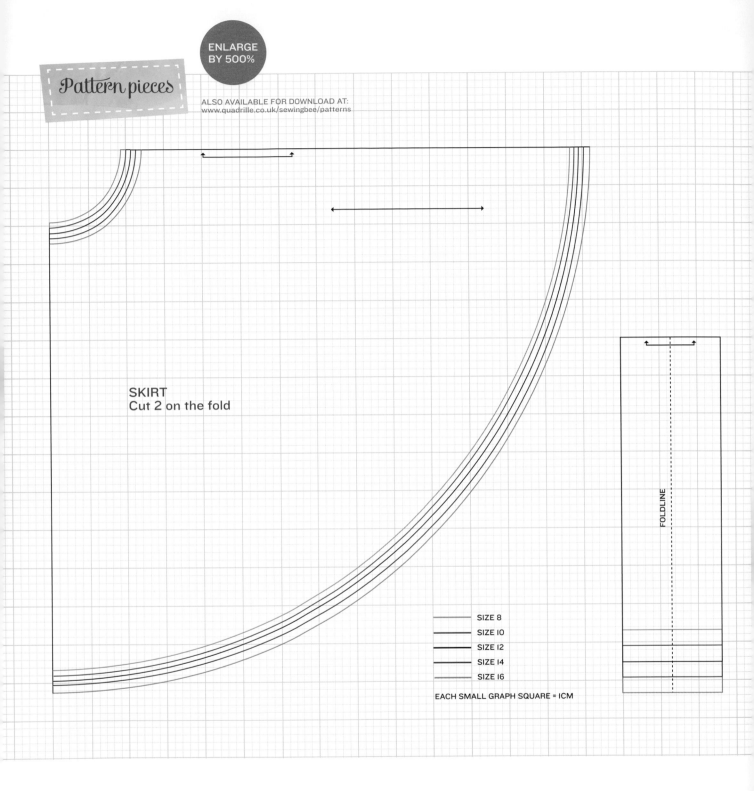

ENLARGE
BY 500%

Pattern pieces

ALSO AVAILABLE FOR DOWNLOAD AT:
www.quadrille.co.uk/sewingbee/patterns

SKIRT
Cut 2 on the fold

FOLDLINE

	SIZE 8
	SIZE 10
	SIZE 12
	SIZE 14
	SIZE 16

EACH SMALL GRAPH SQUARE = 1CM

Cutting diagram

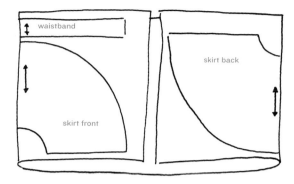

Cutting guide

Press the fabric thoroughly before cutting.

FROM THE MAIN FABRIC:

✄ Cut two skirt pieces, each on the fold – one is for the back and one is for the front.

✄ Cut one piece for the waistband, on the fold. A 1.5cm (⅝in) seam allowance is included on all the pattern pieces, and a 1.5cm (⅝in) hem allowance on the bottom edges of the skirt front and back.

To make the circular skirt

1 STITCH THE SIDE SEAMS AND INSERT THE ZIP
With right sides together, pin the front to the back along the side seams. On the left seam, measure down 24.5cm (9⅝in) from the top edge and mark with a pin. Tack and machine stitch this seam from the pin marker to the hemline. Then insert the invisible zip into the opening at the top of the seam. Tack and stitch the remaining seam all the way from the top to the bottom. Finish the raw seam edges.

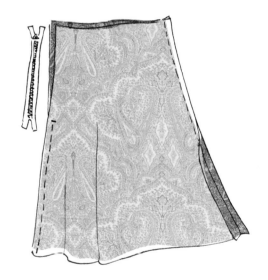

2 PREPARE THE WAISTBAND
With right sides together, fold the waistband piece in half lengthways and machine stitch along both short ends, 1.5cm (⅝in) from the edge. Snip off the corners, trim the seams and press open. Turn the waistband right side out and press the whole waistband in half lengthways.

3 STITCH ON THE WAISTBAND

With right sides together, pin the waistband to the waistline of the skirt, starting at the back edge of the zip. Continue pinning the waistband in place until you reach the front edge of the zip. There will be an extra 1.5cm (⅝in) of waistband remaining for the buttonhole overlap on the skirt front. Tack and stitch the waistband to the skirt. Press the seam open, and then upwards inside the waistband. Firmly press the waistband along the lengthways fold, then, working on the inside of the skirt, fold in the raw edge, including along the overlap. Pin in position and tack. Slipstitch together the folded edges of the overlap.

Then, working from the front side of the skirt, topstitch through all the layers 3mm (⅛in) from the waist seamline and the same distance from the edge of the overlap.

4 MAKE THE BUTTONHOLES

Mark two buttonholes on the overlap and machine stitch. Sew the buttons into the corresponding positions at the other end of the waistband.

5 HEM THE SKIRT

Because of the shape of a circular skirt, if you tried to stitch a normal 5cm (2in) deep blind hem, you'd need to accommodate a lot of extra fabric, which would result in unsightly gathers and puckers. For this reason, circular skirts are always finished with a short hem, normally by machine. At the hem edge, press in 5mm (¼in) to the wrong side all along the bottom edge, then repeat, turning up 1cm (⅜in) to make a double hem, press and tack. Machine stitch this double hem close to the first fold.

Try this...

To give the waistband added stiffness, cut a piece of iron-on interfacing to the length of the waistband and half its width, then press it onto the front half of the band. When finishing the waistband, with the right side facing up, sew around all four sides, including the upper edge.

TEA DRESS

Ultimately feminine, ultimately flattering, with its soft and wide V neckline, this take-you-anywhere tea dress is surprisingly easy to make.

DIFFICULTY RATING:

Materials
1.9m fabric (2¼yd) of 140cm- (55in-) wide synthetic silk fabric or 2.6m (3yd) of 115cm- (45in-) wide fabric
Matching invisible zip, 24cm (10in) long
Matching sewing thread
Four 18mm (¾in) buttons

The hallmark pretty prints, flattering cuts that fit yet flow and feminine details like sweetheart necklines, have ensured that the 1940s-style tea dress remains a vintage favourite. What we know as the tea dress is rooted in the late Victorian 'tea length dress', which could be anything from knee length to mid calf, designed to take you comfortably from day into early evening. Length isn't such an issue these days, but the principle of a pretty, essentially feminine piece that can be worn plain and simple in the day and dressed up for the evening still holds true. This dress with its flattering wide-cut neckline, softly flowing skirt and button detail shoulders is an easy-to-make basic.

TEA DRESS SIZES
To fit UK women's sizes 8, 10, 12, 14 and 16.

FABRIC FINDER
Softly flowing silk works well with the feminine style of the dress, skimming the hips and providing movement in the skirt.
Try these alternatives:
Soft fine cotton—Silk—Silky crepe—Challis—Fine jersey

SKILLS SET
Working even slipstitch **see page 48**—Slipstitching double-fold hems **see page 50**
Stitching straight seams **see page 51**—Clipping curved seams **see page 52**
Finishing seams **see pages 54 and 55**—Easing **see page 63**
Inserting an invisible zip **see pages 68 and 69**—Adding buttons **see page 73**

138

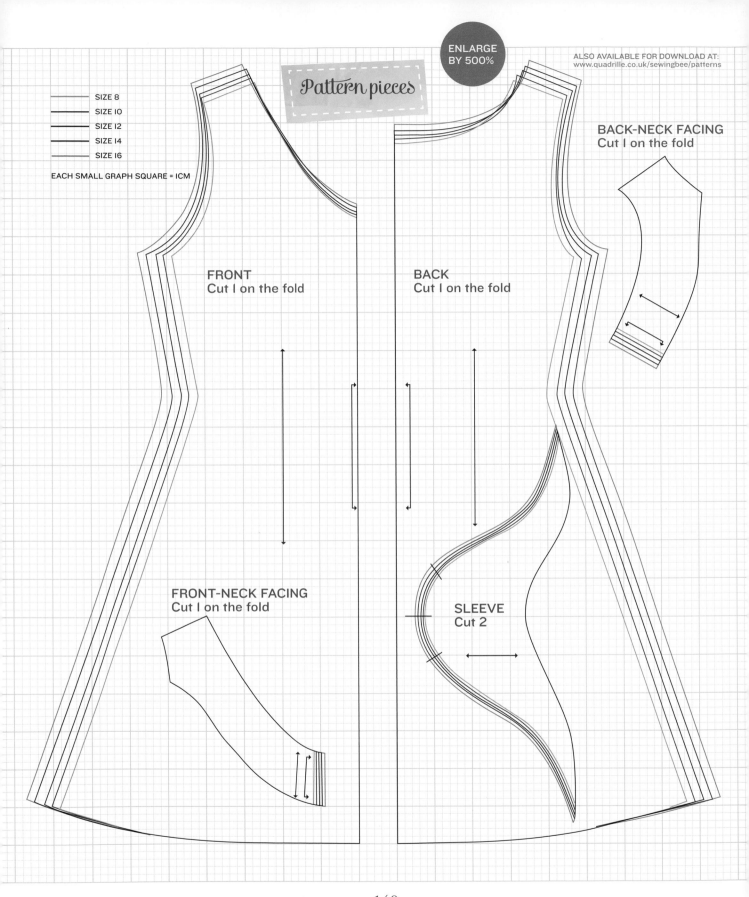

ENLARGE BY 500%

ALSO AVAILABLE FOR DOWNLOAD AT:
www.quadrille.co.uk/sewingbee/patterns

Pattern pieces

SIZE 8
SIZE 10
SIZE 12
SIZE 14
SIZE 16

EACH SMALL GRAPH SQUARE = 1CM

FRONT
Cut 1 on the fold

BACK
Cut 1 on the fold

BACK-NECK FACING
Cut 1 on the fold

FRONT-NECK FACING
Cut 1 on the fold

SLEEVE
Cut 2

140

Cutting diagram

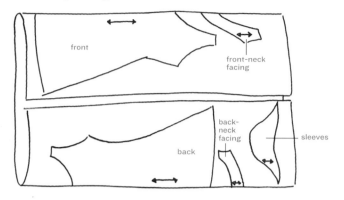

front

front-neck
facing

back-neck
facing

sleeves

back

Cutting guide

Press the fabric carefully before cutting.

FROM THE FABRIC:

✀ Cut one dress front, one dress back, one front-neck facing and one back-neck facing, each on the fold.

✀ Cut two sleeves.

A 1.5cm (⅝in) seam allowance is included on all the pattern pieces, and a 2cm (¾in) hem allowance on the bottom edges of the dress front and back.

To make the tea dress

1 STITCH THE SHOULDER SEAMS
Place the front and back dress pieces with the right sides together and machine stitch the shoulder seams. Then press the seams open. Finish the raw seam edges on dress seams that will be left exposed as you proceed.

2 PREPARE THE FACING
Stitch together the shoulder seams of the facing pieces, then press them open. Next, make a small hem on the outside edge of the facing. Do this by firmly pressing 1cm (⅜in) to the wrong side, then machine stitching.

3 STITCH ON THE FACING
Turn the dress right side out and place the facing right side down around the neckline. Align the raw edges and stitch. Cut a V-notch out of the seam at the point of the V-neck. Clip the curves. Press the seams open, then press the facing to the inside of the dress. Secure the facing in position with a couple of small hand stitches at each shoulder seam.

Try this...

It is much easier to fit sleeves into the armhole before sewing sleeve and side seams, so do it if possible. If you leave the sleeve seams to last and stitch them together at the same time as the dress side seams, everything is guaranteed to lie flat.
MAY MARTIN

4 PREPARE THE SLEEVES

Press under 1cm (⅜in) twice along the bottom edge of each sleeve and stitch this double hem in place close to the first fold. At the shoulder edge, run one or two lines of gathering stitches between the markers. Mark the centre of the sleeve top with a pin.

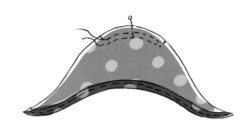

5 STITCH ON THE SLEEVES

Turn the dress inside out. Now pin the right side of the sleeve to the right side of the dress, matching the pin at the top of the sleeve with the shoulder seam, and pin in position. Pull up the gathering threads so the top of the sleeve fits the top of the armhole. Pin the flat underarm part of the sleeve in position. Stitch. Press the seams open. Repeat with the other sleeve.

6 INSERT THE INVISIBLE ZIP

Position the zip in the left side seam between the front and back, so the top of the teeth align with the sleeve hem edge. Insert the zip following the instructions on pages 68–69. Stitch the seam from the bottom of the zip to the hemline and press the seam open. To neaten the ends of the zip tapes, fold the tops under and slipstitch in place.

7 STITCH THE RIGHT SIDE SEAM

Now stitch the right side seam from the hem, all the way up the side and along the short length of the underarm sleeve seam. Press the seam open.

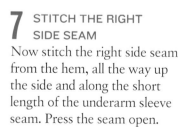

8 HEM THE DRESS AND SEW ON THE BUTTONS

At the hemline, turn up and machine stitch a 1cm (⅜in) double hem. Then sew two buttons to the dress front just below each shoulder seam.

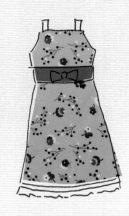

GIRL'S DRESS

Parents love to see their daughters in pretty dresses, so imagine the sense of pride if you have made that dress yourself. Sewing children's clothing is a great way to practise techniques without wasting too much fabric if it goes wrong.

DIFFICULTY RATING: ⊞ ⊞ ⊞ ⊞ ⊞

Materials

- 90cm (1yd) of a 140cm- (55in-) wide cotton print or 1.4m (1²⁄₃yd) of a 115cm- (45in-) wide fabric
- 1.3m (1½yd) of contrasting double satin ribbon, 3.5cm (1³⁄₈in) wide, for waist trim and bow (bow is optional)
- 2m (2¼yd) of 2cm- (¾in-) wide decorative brocade ribbon with a scalloped edge, for straps and hem edging
- White tulle, enough to make a 6cm- (2¼in-) wide strip 3m (3⅓yd) long, for hem edging
- Matching invisible zip 16cm (6½in) long
- 3 button moulds for 12mm (½in) covered buttons (optional)
- Sewing thread to match fabric and ribbon

With no sleeves to set in and pretty jacquard ribbon used as straps, this dress is not only easy to make, but can 'grow' with your child. Cut the straps a little long and leave the extra length behind the facing. If she's grown by next year, just undo a couple of stitches where it is sewn into the garment, lengthen the straps then re-sew. This design shows you the neatest way to add frills and ribbon to the hemline.

GIRL'S DRESS SIZES
To fit child 2–3 years, 4–5 years, 5–6 years and 7–8 years.

FABRIC FINDER
Printed cottons like this are always a good choice as they look pretty and are easy to sew. You can create a completely different look by using an alternative but co-ordinated fabric for the bodice.
Try these alternatives:
Gingham—Seersucker—Calico—Fine cotton lawn—Chambray

SKILLS SET
Working even slipstitch see page 48
Stitching straight seams see page 51—Clipping curved seams
see page 52—Finishing seams see pages 54 and 55
Inserting an invisible zip see pages 68 and 69

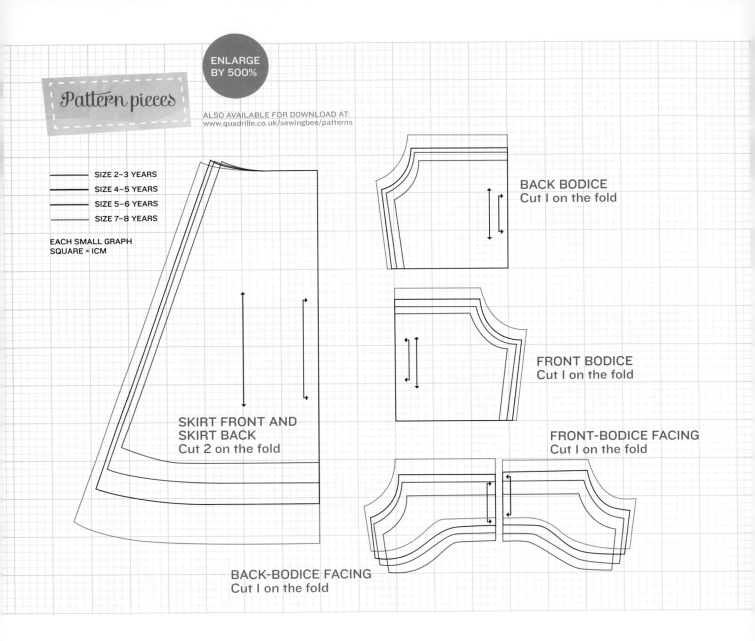

ALSO AVAILABLE FOR DOWNLOAD AT: www.quadrille.co.uk/sewingbee/patterns

ENLARGE
BY 500%

Pattern pieces

— SIZE 2–3 YEARS
— SIZE 4–5 YEARS
— SIZE 5–6 YEARS
— SIZE 7–8 YEARS

EACH SMALL GRAPH
SQUARE = 1CM

BACK BODICE
Cut I on the fold

FRONT BODICE
Cut I on the fold

FRONT-BODICE FACING
Cut I on the fold

**SKIRT FRONT AND
SKIRT BACK**
Cut 2 on the fold

BACK-BODICE FACING
Cut I on the fold

Cutting diagram

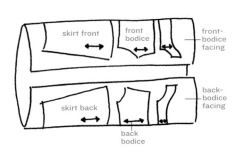

skirt front

front
bodice

front-
bodice
facing

skirt back

back-
bodice
facing

back
bodice

Cutting guide

Press the fabric thoroughly before cutting.

FROM THE FABRIC:

✂ Cut two skirts, one front bodice, one back bodice, one front-bodice facing, one back-bodice facing, each on the fold.

A 1.5cm (⅝in) seam allowance is included on all the pattern pieces, and a 3cm (1¼in) hem allowance on the skirt front and back.

To make the girl's dress

1 STITCH THE BODICE PIECES TO THE SKIRT PIECES
With right sides together, stitch the bodice front to the skirt front and the bodice back to the skirt back. Finish the raw seam edges and press the seams open.

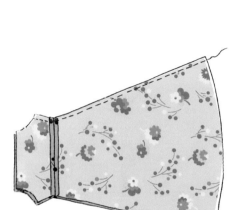

2 STITCH THE RIGHT SIDE SEAM
With right sides together, stitch the right dress side-seam. Finish the raw seam edges and press the seams open.

3 STITCH ON THE SATIN RIBBON
Using tailor's chalk, and a steel straight edge, mark a line 1cm (⅜in) above and 2.5cm (1in) below the waist seamline on the right side of the dress. Using these guidelines, pin the ribbon to the waist, starting at the dress's left side-seam, working across the back and around to the front until you get to the left side-seam again. Tack and then, using a zip foot, topstitch it in place as close to the edges of the ribbon as possible. Remove the tacking.

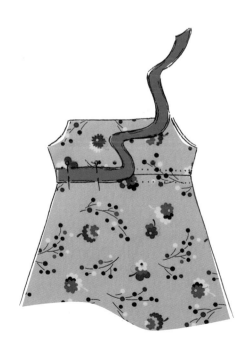

4 STITCH ONE FACING SIDE SEAM
Place the front-bodice facing on the front bodice and the back-bodice facing on the back bodice, with right sides together. Then pin together the same facing side-seam as the side-seam that is stitched on the bodice, with right sides together. Take the facing off the bodice, and tack and stitch the pinned seam. Remove the tacking and press the seam open.

5 STITCH ON THE FACINGS AND RIBBON STRAPS

Cut two pieces of the scallop-edged brocade ribbon for the shoulder straps, each measuring 30cm (12in) long. Next, with right sides together, pin one end of each shoulder strap 1.5cm (⅝in) from the top corners of the front bodice. Now pin the other ends of the straps to the back bodice so they each measure 18cm (7in) long. Leave extra ribbon for future adjustments. With right sides together, lay the prepared facing on top of the bodice over the straps. Starting and ending at the open side seam, stitch the facing in place along the armhole and neck edges. Snip the corners and clip the curves. Press the seams open, then press the facings to the inside of the dress and press the folded seam edge.

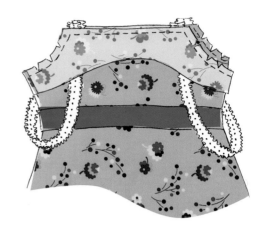

6 INSERT THE ZIP

On the left side-seam, mark the end of the zip position with a pin. Insert the invisible zip and stitch the side seam. Take care to stitch the zip to the dress only and leave the facing free. Press the seam open.

7 SLIPSTITCH THE FACING ENDS

Turn in one end of the facing at the zip and slipstitch it to the zip tape to finish. Repeat with the other end.

8 TURN UP THE HEM EDGE

Press 1cm (⅜in) to the wrong side along the hem edge. Machine stitch this turning in place.

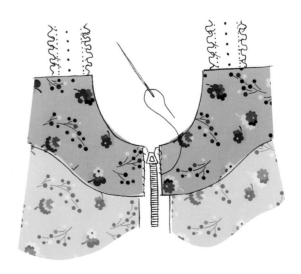

148

9 PREPARE THE RIBBON AND TULLE EDGING

Cut a length of decorative scallop-edged brocade ribbon 5cm (2in) longer than the hem edge of the dress. Next, cut a 3m (3¼yd) length of tulle 6cm (2¼in) wide. Run gathering stitches along one long side, 6mm (¼in) from one edge. Pin the gathered tulle to the top edge of the wrong side of the ribbon, positioning the line of gathering stitches 3mm (⅛in) below the top edge of the ribbon. Then tack and stitch the tulle to the ribbon 3mm (⅛in) from the top edge of the ribbon.

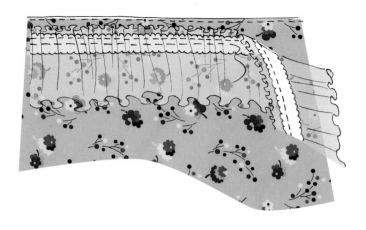

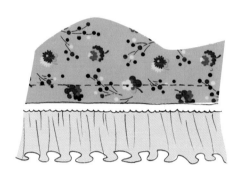

10 STITCH THE EDGING TO THE DRESS

With the dress right side out, lay it upside down so the hem edge is at the top. Starting at one side-seam, pin the prepared ribbon-and-tulle edging right side down on the right side of the skirt, with the gathered edge of the tulle at the top and the centre of the ribbon precisely 2cm (¾in) from the hemline edge. When the edging is pinned in position, turn in the ends so they align with the seam and stitch them together. Machine stitch the edging in place, stitching exactly 2cm (¾in) from the hem edge (along the centre of the ribbon).

11 COMPLETE THE HEM

Fold the hem to the wrong side along the edging seam, so half the scalloped ribbon and the tulle frill peek out below the hem. Machine stitch the turned-up hem. Press, avoiding the tulle.

12 MAKE THE BOW

To make the decorative double bow for the centre front of the dress, cut two lengths of satin ribbon, one 15cm (6in) long and one 19cm (7½in) long. Overlap the end of the shortest ribbon by 1cm (½in) and hand sew the overlap together with a couple of stitches. Pinch this ring of ribbon together at the centre, with the overlap at the centre of one side and stitch it together with a couple of hand stitches to form a 7cm (2¾in) bow. Make a 9cm (3½in) bow in the same way with the longer length of ribbon. Place the shorter bow on top of the longer bow, wrap the bow centre with a short length of ribbon and sew this length together on the wrong side of the bow. Stitch the bow to the ribbon at the centre front of the dress.

Try this…

As an alternative to the bow, you could decorate the front bodice with three little fabric-covered buttons. Cover the buttons with the dress fabric, then sew them to the bodice front in a little line, between the neck edge and the satin ribbon. MAY MARTIN

TIE CUSHION

With no zips or buttonholes, this cushion is one of the easiest makes in the book. Choosing a contrast lining and ties adds style to this otherwise plain cushion. With this simple design, it's possible to create an entire set of cushions in an afternoon.

DIFFICULTY RATING: ⊞ ⊞ ⊞ ⊞ ⊞

Super simple to make, if you can stitch in a straight line, you'll be able to make this elegant cushion cover with ties. There's no tricky zip to contend with and the ties are something of a trimming in themselves. The charm of the design lies in the flash of colour from the lining, which can be seen due to the pillowcase-like construction of the cover. Aside from contrasting colours, the two fabrics used have contrasting textures as well – the outer fabric is a soft-to-the-touch furnishing fabric and the lining a shiny slubbed silk.

CUSHION SIZE
The finished cushion measures 45 x 45cm (17¾ x 17¾in).

FABRIC FINDER
Scatter cushions can be made in almost any fabric, though furnishing fabrics are more durable and will withstand more wear and tear. The outside of this one is made from firm brushed upholstery cotton with a lining in slubbed silk.
Try these alternatives:
Furnishing cotton—Furnishing linen and linen blends—Linen blends—Furnishing silk—Jacquard—Dupion—Tapestries—Chintz

Materials
60cm (²/₃yd) of a medium-weight closely woven fabric at least 115cm (45in) wide, for main fabric
35cm (½yd) of raw silk at least 112cm (44in) wide, for lining fabric
Matching sewing thread
Cushion pad to fit finished cover

SKILLS SET
Stitching straight seams **see page 51**—Finishing seams **see pages 54 and 55**

Cutting guide

Press the fabric thoroughly before cutting. Measure and mark the fabric carefully using a steel rule and ensure all the corners are at perfect right angles before cutting.

FROM THE MAIN FABRIC:

✂ Cut one outer cover piece, measuring 92 x 47cm (36½ x 18¾in)

✂ Cut four strips for the ties, each 6 x 26.5cm (2½ x 10½in)

FROM THE CONTRASTING LINING FABRIC:

✂ Cut two lining pieces, each 25 x 47cm (10¼ x 18¾in)

✂ Cut four strips for the ties, each 6 x 26.5cm (2½ x 10½in)

To make the tie cushion

1 PREPARE THE TIES

With right sides together, place a lining-fabric tie strip on top of a main-fabric tie strip, then snip off a 45-degree triangle of fabric right at one end of the strips. Pin the strips together, then machine stitch up one long edge, along the diagonal and down the other long edge, using a 1cm (⅜in) seam allowance. Leave the straight end unstitched. Snip off the angled point, being careful not to cut the stitches. Press the seams open, turn right side out and press again. Prepare the remaining three ties in the same way. Be sure to shape the tie ends in the same way so the angled ends all slant in the same direction.

2 PREPARE THE LINING PIECES

Along one long side of each lining piece, fold under 1cm (⅜in) twice and press to form a double hem. Machine stitch the hem in place close to the first fold.

3 STITCH ON THE LINING PIECES

Lay the main fabric piece right side up on a flat surface. On the short ends of the piece, measure and mark with pins the positions for the ties, centred and 11cm (4¼in) apart. Pin the ties in place, with the main fabric on the ties facing the main fabric piece and with the raw edges aligned. With the right sides together, place a lining piece on top of the ties at each end of the main piece. Using a 1cm (⅜in) seam allowance, stitch through all layers, so catching in the ties. Press the seams open. If you think the raw edges of your fabrics will unravel easily, finish the raw edges of the seams you have just stitched.

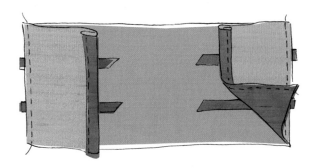

4 STITCH SIDE SEAMS

Fold the whole piece in half widthways, aligning the lining seams, and pin and stitch all along both side seams, again taking a 1cm (⅜in) seam. Press the seams open.

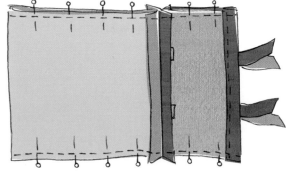

5 ADD THE FINISHING TOUCHES

Finish the raw edges of the side seams if desired. Then turn the cover right side out and push the lining inside the cover. Press thoroughly. Put the cushion pad into the cover, tucking it under one side of the lining – just like you would in a pillowcase. Lastly, tie the ties neatly together.

COOK'S APRON

Easy to sew, aprons are often the first projects taught at beginners' classes. With no fiddly fastenings or shapings to deal with, only straight seams, gathering and ties, an apron affords plenty of practice with basic sewing skills.

DIFFICULTY RATING: ⊞ ⊞ ⊞ ⊞ ⊞

Materials

70cm (⅞yd) of a 140cm-(55in-) wide cotton duck print, for main fabric

40cm (½yd) of a 140cm-(55in-) wide contrasting plain cotton duck, for neck straps, waistband, waist ties and frill

40 x 60cm (16 x 24in) of a cotton lining fabric

2.7m (3yd) ready-made 12mm- (½in-) wide bias binding

Matching sewing thread

This apron is almost a sampler of key sewing skills – gathering, putting on a waistband, making a lined bib, even adding frills and bias. But as it's essentially flat with no complicated shaping or fastenings, there's little to go wrong. This project makes a great homemade gift for cook's of all ages.

APRON SIZE
The finished apron is approximately 90cm (35½in) long, from the top of the bib to the bottom of the frill.

FABRIC FINDER
The cotton duck used for this apron is a medium-weight canvas-type fabric. It is closely woven: good for protecting clothing from oily cooking splashes.
Try these alternatives:
Gingham—Cotton prints—Calico—Chambray

SKILLS SET
Working even slipstitch see page 48—Stitching straight seams see page 51
Clipping curved seams see page 52—Finishing seams see pages 54 and 55
Hand gathering see page 62—Applying bias binding see page 71

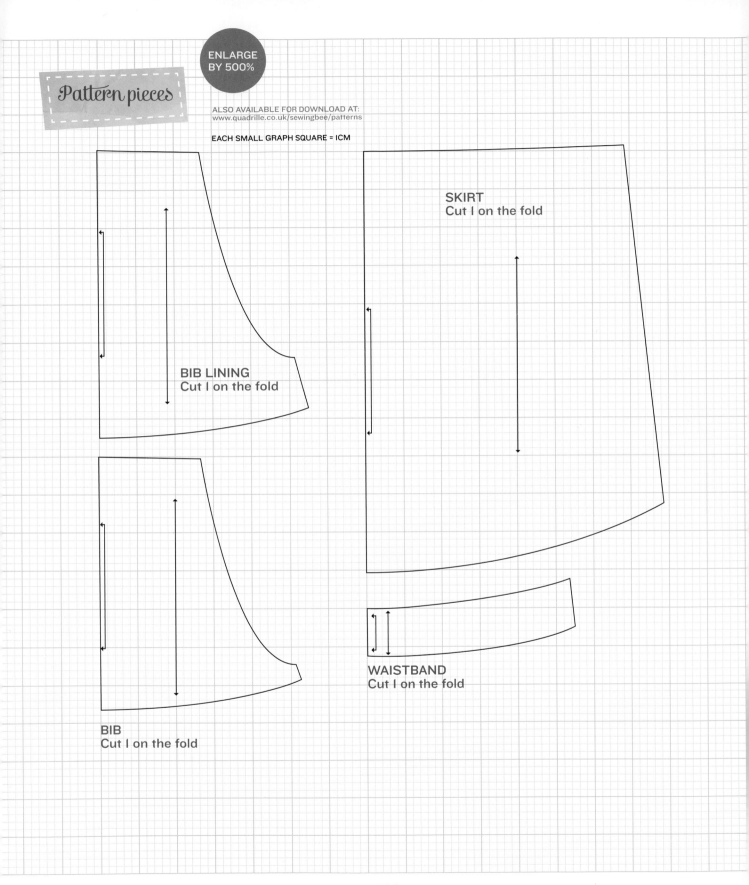

ENLARGE
BY 500%

Pattern pieces

ALSO AVAILABLE FOR DOWNLOAD AT:
www.quadrille.co.uk/sewingbee/patterns

EACH SMALL GRAPH SQUARE = ICM

SKIRT
Cut I on the fold

BIB LINING
Cut I on the fold

BIB
Cut I on the fold

WAISTBAND
Cut I on the fold

Cutting diagrams

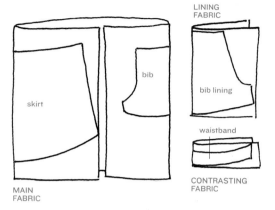

LINING
FABRIC

bib

bib lining

skirt

waistband

MAIN
FABRIC

CONTRASTING
FABRIC

Cutting guide

Press the fabric thoroughly before cutting.

FROM THE MAIN FABRIC:

✂ Cut one skirt and one bib, both on the fold.

FROM THE CONTRASTING FABRIC:

✂ Cut one waistband, on the fold.

✂ Cut one strip for the frill, measuring 6 x 140cm (2⅜in x 55in).

✂ Cut two strips for the waist ties, each 8 x 84cm (3¼in x 33in).

✂ Cut two strips for the neck straps, each 8 x 58cm (3¼in x 22¾in).

FROM THE LINING FABRIC:

✂ Cut one bib lining, on the fold.

A 1cm (⅜in) seam allowance is included on all the pattern pieces.

To make the apron

1 PREPARE THE NECK STRAPS AND WAIST TIES
Fold one of the waist ties in half lengthways and press. Trim one end of the folded strip at a 45-degree angle to create a diagonal end. Using a 1cm (⅜in) seam allowance, stitch along the long edge and the diagonal end, leaving the end of the tie open. Clip off the point of the seam allowance at the shaped end and turn the tie right side out. Prepare the remaining waist tie and both neck straps in the same way.

2 SEW THE WAISTBAND TO THE BIB
With right sides together, stitch the waistband to the lower edge of the bib. Press the seam open, then press it away from the bib. It is important to press the seam downwards so it isn't in the way of the lining seam in the next step.

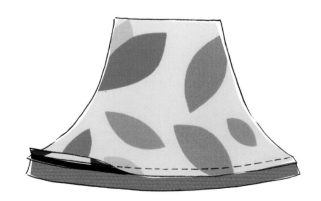

157

3 LINE THE BIB
Place the bib right side up on a flat surface. With raw edges aligned, pin a neck strap just inside the seam allowance at either side of the top edge of the bib. Now lay the bib lining right side down on top of the straps and pin, aligning the edges with the bib piece below. Stitch through all layers along the top and from the top down to the waistband on each side. Be sure to stitch right up to the waistband seam, but do not stitch into the waistband. Clip off the corners and trim the seams. Press the seams open and turn right side out.

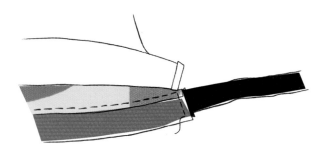

4 SEW ON THE WAIST TIES
At one end of the waistband, pin one waist tie to the side edge of the waistband, with right sides together and with the tie seam facing downwards. Stitch the tie to the waistband – make sure this seam is aligned with the end of the bib-and-lining seam. Press the seam towards the waistband. Repeat with the other waist tie. Leave the lining loose at the waist, it will be slipstitched in place after the skirt is added on.

5 STITCH ON THE SKIRT FRILL
At the hem edge, with right sides together, pin the contrasting frill strip onto the apron skirt, making even pleats about 4cm (1½in) wide with a 1cm (⅜in) return. Take your time and adjust the pleats until you're happy they're as even as possible – they don't have to be perfect. Tack the frill in place, then stitch 1cm (⅜in) from the edge. Remove the tacking and press the seam toward the skirt. To neaten the seam, finish the raw edges with machine zigzag or overlocking stitches.

6 BIND THE EDGES OF THE SKIRT AND FRILL

Next, cover the raw edges of the frill and the side edges of the skirt with ready-made bias binding. Starting at one side edge of the skirt, pin and tack the binding in place down the side of the skirt, along the side of the frill, across the bottom of the frill and up the other side of the frill and skirt. Stitch the binding close to its edge. Remove the tacking and press.

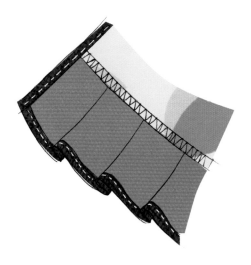

7 SEW THE BIB AND SKIRT TOGETHER

Run gathering stitches along 34cm (13½in) at the centre of the top edge of the skirt. With right sides together, pin the skirt to the lower edge of the waistband, drawing the gathers up to fit the waistband. Tack and stitch. Remove the tacking and press the seam upwards.

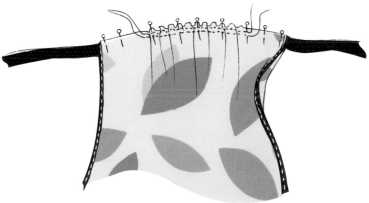

8 SLIPSTITCH THE LINING IN PLACE

On the reverse, turn in the raw edges of the lining where the waist ties are stitched on. Then turn in the raw edge along the bottom of the lining, aligning the fold with the bottom of the waistband and pin. Slipstitch all along to finish.

159

PROM DRESS

This 1950s-inspired dress with its simple halter neckline, takes on the style of a classic prom dress. Having mastered the art of boning, you'll be able to tackle any special occasion outfit. Make the dress in spotted cotton for everyday wear or satin for evening wear or a bridesmaid's dress.

DIFFICULTY RATING: 🔘 🔘 🔘 🔘 ⬤

Making a boned bodice might be daunting, but if you take your time and follow the steps, it's surprisingly easy and ultimately very satisfying. The trick is to make sure you seam the pieces together accurately, in the right order and the right way up. This boned bodice has been designed with relatively few pieces so even beginners can get to grips with the method without going wrong.

PROM DRESS SIZES
To fit UK women's sizes 8, 10, 12, 14 and 16.

FABRIC FINDER
A crisp cotton with a navy ground and white polka dots was chosen for this dress. Fabric with a little body gives the circular skirt a stand-out flare, but a more flimsy or more slinky fabric would suit the design just as well. You could make your first version in cotton and progress to silk for the next.
Try these alternatives:
Fine cotton prints—Raw silk—Silky crepe—Fine jersey

Materials
- 2.4m (2⅔yd) of 140cm-(55in-) wide fabric, or 3.4m (3¾yd) of 115cm-(45in-) wide fabric
- 60 x 70cm (24 x 28in) woven iron-on interfacing
- 1.5m (1½yd) of cotton covered boning
- 1.2m (1⅓yd) of grosgrain ribbon 3cm (1¼in) wide, for the belt
- 46cm (18in) invisible zip
- Matching sewing thread

SKILLS SET
Working even slipstitching see page 48—Slipstitching double-fold hems see page 50
Stitching straight seams see page 51—Clipping curved seams see page 52
Finishing seams see pages 54 and 55—Inserting an invisible zip see pages 68 and 69

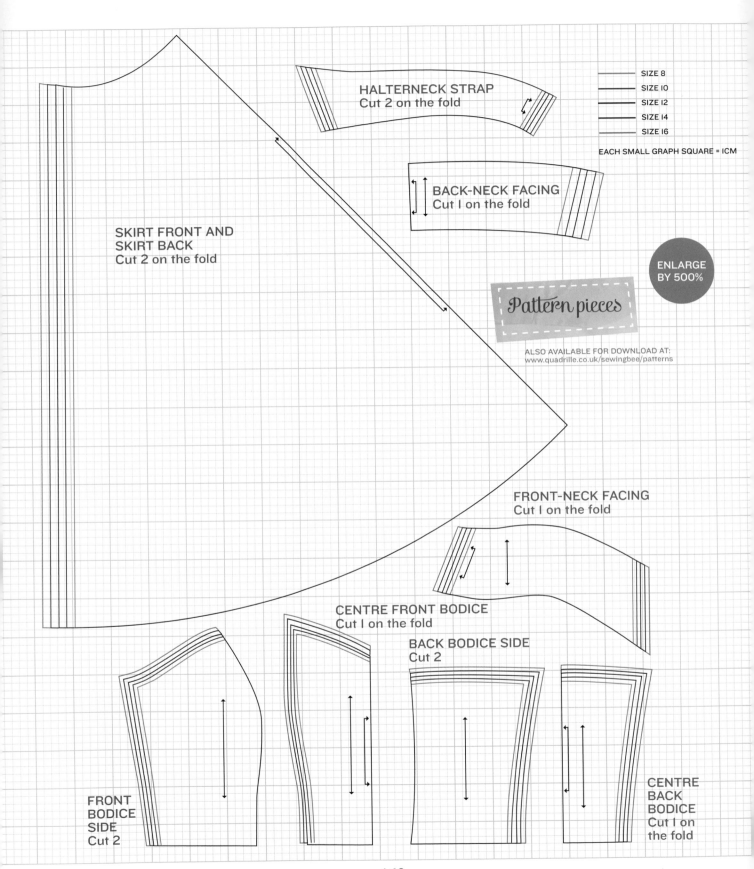

HALTERNECK STRAP
Cut 2 on the fold

SIZE 8
SIZE 10
SIZE 12
SIZE 14
SIZE 16

EACH SMALL GRAPH SQUARE = 1CM

BACK-NECK FACING
Cut 1 on the fold

SKIRT FRONT AND
SKIRT BACK
Cut 2 on the fold

ENLARGE
BY 500%

Pattern pieces

ALSO AVAILABLE FOR DOWNLOAD AT:
www.quadrille.co.uk/sewingbee/patterns

FRONT-NECK FACING
Cut 1 on the fold

CENTRE FRONT BODICE
Cut 1 on the fold

BACK BODICE SIDE
Cut 2

FRONT
BODICE
SIDE
Cut 2

CENTRE
BACK
BODICE
Cut 1 on
the fold

Cutting diagrams

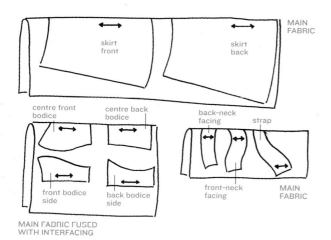

skirt
front

skirt
back

MAIN
FABRIC

centre front
bodice

centre back
bodice

back-neck
facing

strap

front bodice
side

back bodice
side

front-neck
facing

MAIN
FABRIC

MAIN FABRIC FUSED
WITH INTERFACING

Cutting guide

Press the fabric thoroughly before cutting.

FROM THE FABRIC:

✄ Cut two skirts, one back-neck facing, one front-neck facing and two halterneck straps, each on the fold.

FROM THE FABRIC FUSED WITH INTERFACING:

Press the iron-on interfacing onto the wrong side of a rectangle of fabric measuring 60 x 70cm (24 x 28in). Fold this interfaced piece in half widthways.

✄ Cut one centre front bodice and one centre back bodice, both on the fold.

✄ Cut two back bodice sides and two front bodice sides. The 1.5cm (⅝in) seam allowances and a 5cm (2in) hem allowance are included in the pattern pieces.

To make the prom dress

1 PREPARE THE HALTERNECK STRAP

With right sides together, match the two halterneck strap pieces. Stitch along the long edges, leaving the ends open. Trim the seams and clip the curves. Turn the strap right side out and press.

2 PREPARE THE FRONT AND BACK BODICE

With right sides together, stitch the left front bodice to the centre front bodice and then the right front bodice to the centre front bodice. Repeat this process with the back bodice pieces. To prepare for boning, press the seams open using plenty of pressure and steam. For boning, it is important they are pressed fully open and flat.

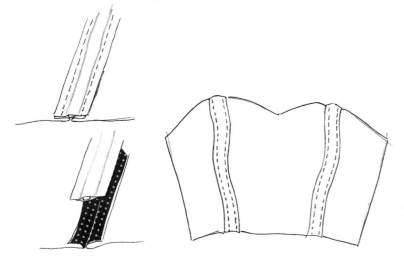

3 ADD THE BONING TO FRONT AND BACK BODICE

Cut a piece of boning to the length of each seam just stitched, then snip 4cm (1½in) off one end of each (this is to allow for seam allowances). Pin and tack the boning to the seam allowances, ensuring each piece lies just short of the seam allowance at the top and bottom of the seam. The boning is stitched to the seam allowances so the stitching lines do not show on the right side of the dress. Use a zip foot to stitch as close as possible to each boning edge.

4 STITCH THE BODICE AND THE SKIRT
With right sides together, stitch the front bodice and back bodice together along the right side-seam. In the same way, stitch the right side-seam of the skirt. Press the seams open.

5 JOIN THE BODICE TO THE SKIRT
With right sides together and raw edges meeting, stitch the skirt to the bodice, matching the side-seam of the bodice to the side-seam of the skirt. Press the seam open, then press it upwards. Finish the raw edges.

6 INSERT THE ZIP AND SEW THE HEM
Insert the invisible zip into the left side-seam of the dress, then stitch the remaining seam from the bottom of the zip to the hemline. Turn up and stitch a 2.5cm (1in) double hem.

7 SEW ON THE NECK FACING AND STRAP
With right sides together, stitch the front and back neck facing pieces together along the right side-seam. Press the seam open. Turn up and press 1cm (⅜in) along the lower edge of facing. Stitch in place. With raw edges aligned, pin the halterneck strap to the right side of the bodice, so the inside strap seam aligns on either side with the outside centre front seams of the bodice. Now place the prepared facing right side down top of this, matching the right side-seam and the curved edges of the front. Pin, tack and stitch. Trim the seams and press open. Fold the facing to the inside, then turn in the raw edges at each end of the facing and slipstitch close to the zip.

8 STITCH ON THE BELT
Cut the grosgrain to fit the waistline, plus extra for turning under 1cm (⅜in) at each end. Turn under 1cm (⅜in) at each end and pin in position exactly over the waist seam. Hand stitch in place along the short ends using slipstitches – leave the rest of the ribbon loose around the waist.

WINDOW PANEL

This chic alternative to net curtains can be made in sheer white or a bright organza. It's the project to choose if you're meticulous by nature but new to sewing – with a flat panel, you'll get plenty of straight sewing practice, but you must be precise in the cutting.

DIFFICULTY RATING: ⊕ ⊕ ⊕ ⊕ ⊕

Materials

Sheer linen to fit your window (see the Cutting Guide for how much fabric to purchase)

Striped grosgrain ribbon 2.5cm (1in) wide – as long as the width of the finished window panel plus 3cm (1¼in)

Matching sewing thread

Plastic-covered curtain tensile wire with metal eyes and two metal hooks – as long as the width of the window

Wooden dowel 12mm (½in) in diameter – as long as the width of the finished window panel (optional)

Making a sheer panel couldn't be easier as there's no lining or gathering to contend with. However, to make it look smart, you need to be meticulous about how you cut out the fabric, making sure it is absolutely square. A braid can be added to the bottom edge, like the one shown here, or it can be left plain. However, a line of braid provides extra weight and rigidity to keep the panel in shape.

WINDOW PANEL SIZE
The window panel can be made to fit any window size.

FABRIC FINDER
This panel is made in pure cotton voile. Aim to choose a sheer that has some body to it. Synthetics are inclined to be more floppy than natural fibres and are more suited to sheers that are gathered.
Try these alternatives:
Cotton organdie—Sheer linen—Furnishing silk organza

SKILLS SET
Slipstitching double-fold hems **see page 50**

Cutting guide

FROM THE CURTAIN FABRIC:
✂ Cut a piece of fabric that is 16cm (6in) longer and wider than the size of the finished window panel. Sheer fabric is difficult to cut in a straight line, so for really straight edges, first cut the fabric piece 2cm (¾in) longer and 2cm (¾in) wider than the dimensions you have just calculated for your piece of fabric. Then trim it down to the correct size. To do this, carefully pull out one thread along each edge to give you an accurate straight edge. Cut the excess off the frayed edges until you have the exact measurements for the panel.

To make the window panel

1 HEM THE TOP, BOTTOM AND SIDES OF THE PANEL
Fold and press 4cm (1½in) to the wrong side along one vertical edge of the panel, measuring the turning every 10cm (4in) for accuracy. Press 4cm (1½in) to the wrong side again so you have a double hem, and pin. Topstitch the hem 3mm (⅛in) from the first fold, being careful to keep the stitching really straight. Repeat along the other vertical edge. Stitch a 4cm (1½in) double hem along the top and bottom of the panel in the same way for a perfectly formed rectangle.

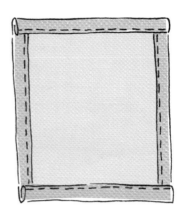

2 CREATE A CHANNEL FOR THE TENSILE WIRE
Add an additional line of stitching along the centre of the hem at the top of the panel, 2cm (¾in) from the top folded edge. This creates a channel below the new line of stitching for the tensile wire.

3 SEW ON THE RIBBON TRIM
Pin the grosgrain ribbon to the right side of the window panel along the bottom hem, aligning the top of the ribbon with the top of the hem. At each end of the ribbon, fold 1.5cm (⅝in) into the inside of the hem. Using a zip foot, stitch the ribbon in place along the top and bottom edges, as close to the edge as possible. This creates a channel in the bottom hem for the wooden dowel if you are using one to weight the panel.

4 HANG THE FINISHED PANEL
Thread the covered tensile wire through the channel created for it at the top of the panel. Screw a screw eye into each end. Screw a hook into the architrave 2cm (¾in) from the top of the window frame so that it is in line with where the tensile wire sits inside the panel channel. Then hang the window panel in position.

5 INSERT THE DOWEL
To weight the panel, slide the wooden dowel into the channel behind the ribbon. There's no need to stitch up the ends as it's unlikely to slip out, yet it can easily be removed when you want to launder the blind.

HACKING JACKET

This classic tweed hacking jacket is a complex project that novice sewers will need to work up to. However, once you have made your own jacket, tailored for a perfect fit, you'll never want to buy one off-the-peg ever again.

DIFFICULTY RATING: ⊞ ⊞ ⊞ ⊞ ⊞

Tailored jackets are not a good choice for beginners. Negotiating notched lapels and set-in sleeves are tasks that require accurate stitching and plenty of experience easing fabric. That said, once you do have sewing experience, making your own jacket gives you the opportunity to make it to perfect-measure. If you were to do this, it's best to follow the example of bespoke tailors and make one up in a toile (calico) to begin with so you can try it on and make adjustments before cutting the fabric. One of the contestants in *The Great British Sewing Bee* chose this New Look pattern for an unlined jacket, which is easier to make than a lined one, but added their own flair with the cute cuffs.

HACKING JACKET SIZES
To fit UK women's sizes 8, 10, 12, 14 and 16.

FABRIC FINDER
This jacket is made in a tweedy wool, perfect for tailoring as it takes shape well and doesn't crease too easily.
Try these alternatives:
Wool—Worsted—Linen—Heavy cotton—Gabardine

SKILLS SET
Working even slipstitch **see page 48**—Stitching straight seams **see page 51**
Clipping curved seams **see page 52**—Finishing seams **see pages 54 and 55**
Grading seams **see page 58**—Making single-point darts **see page 60**
Easing **see page 63**—Making buttonholes **see page 72**—Adding buttons **see page 73**

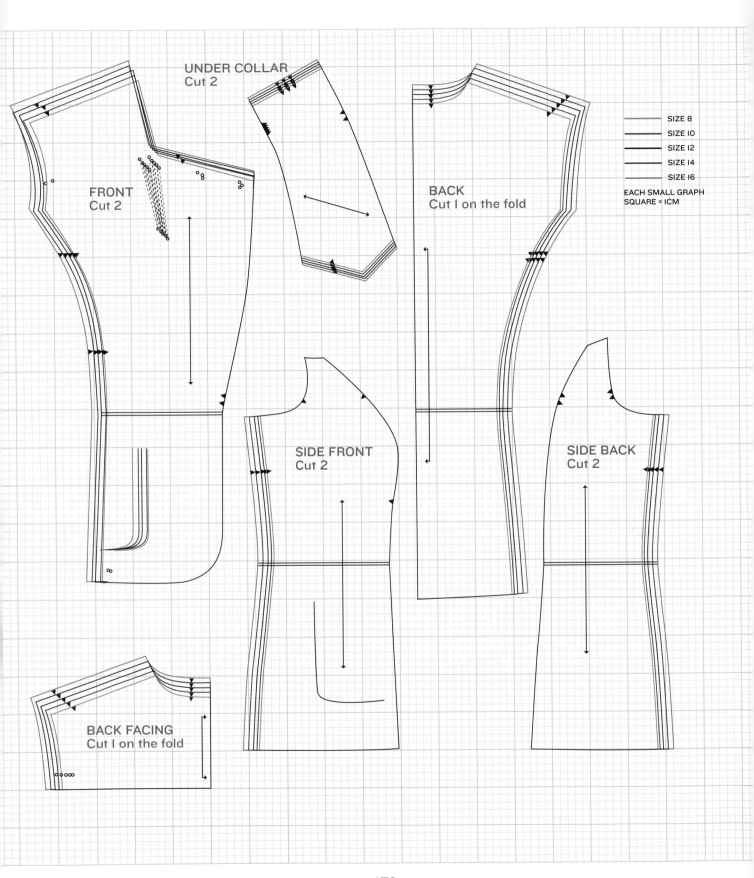

UNDER COLLAR
Cut 2

FRONT
Cut 2

BACK
Cut 1 on the fold

SIZE 8
SIZE 10
SIZE 12
SIZE 14
SIZE 16

EACH SMALL GRAPH
SQUARE = 1CM

SIDE FRONT
Cut 2

SIDE BACK
Cut 2

BACK FACING
Cut 1 on the fold

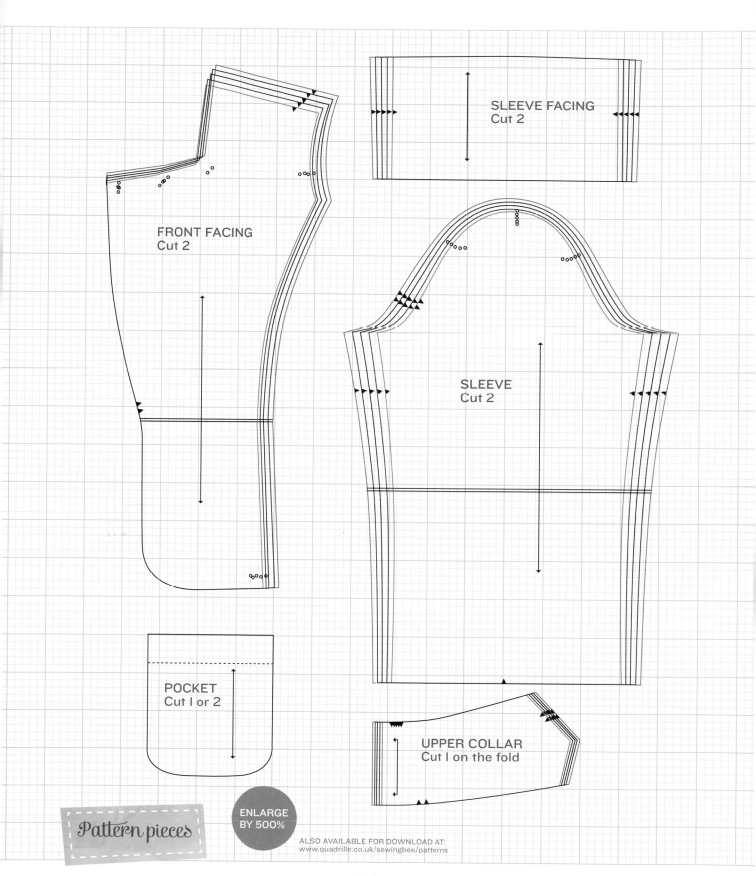

SLEEVE FACING
Cut 2

FRONT FACING
Cut 2

SLEEVE
Cut 2

POCKET
Cut 1 or 2

UPPER COLLAR
Cut 1 on the fold

Pattern pieces

ENLARGE
BY 500%

ALSO AVAILABLE FOR DOWNLOAD AT:
www.quadrille.co.uk/sewingbee/patterns

Cutting guide

Press the fabric thoroughly before cutting.

FROM THE MAIN FABRIC:

✂ Cut two fronts, two side fronts, two side backs, two under collars, two front facings, two sleeves and one or two pockets (as preferred).

✂ Cut one centre back, one upper collar and one back facing, each on the fold.

FROM THE CONTRASTING FABRIC:

✂ Cut two sleeve facings for the lower end of each sleeve.

FROM THE INTERFACING:

✂ Cut two sleeve facings, two under collars and two front facings.

✂ Cut one upper collar and one back facing, both on the fold. Following the manufacturer's instructions, iron the interfacing onto the wrong side of the relevant pieces.

The 1.5cm (⅝in) seam allowances and all hem allowances are included in the pattern pieces.

Cutting diagram

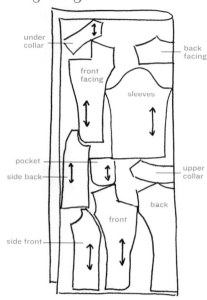

To make the jacket

1 STITCH TOGETHER THE FRONT AND BACK PIECES
With right sides together, stitch the back side pieces to the centre back and one front side piece to each front piece. Press the front seams towards the centre front edges and the back seams towards the centre back. Then stitch the back and front together along the shoulder and side seams. Press these seams open. Finish the raw seam edges as desired.

2 PREPARE THE POCKET
At the upper edge of the pocket, press 6mm (¼in) to the wrong side. Turn this upper edge to the outside along the foldline – about 3cm (1¼in) from the first fold – to form a facing. Stitch around the outer edge of the sides and bottom of the pocket, stitching along the seamline and over the facing at each end. Trim off the corner at the facing without cutting into the stitches. Make a line of gathering stitches inside the seam allowance down one side, along the bottom and up the other side of the pocket. Turn this facing to the wrong side and press. Topstitch along the top of the pocket, close to the first hem fold. Fold the seam allowance to the wrong side along the seamline stitching, pulling up the gathering stitches to ease the fabric at the corners, and pin. Clip the curves where the easing stitches have created fullness. Tack. If you are adding two pockets, do the same with the second pocket.

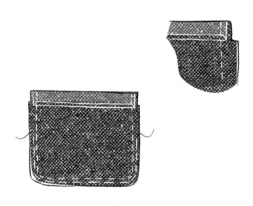

3 STITCH ON THE POCKET

Pin the pocket to the front of the jacket, matching the marks. Topstitch down one side, along the bottom and up the other side of the pocket. Alternatively, slipstitch the pocket in place. If you have a second pocket, repeat.

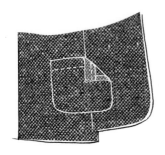

4 STITCH THE ENDS OF THE UNDER COLLAR TO THE LAPELS

Stitch the centre back seam of the under collar. Press the seam open. With right sides together, pin the ends of the under collar to the front neck edge along the lapel, matching the large and small dots. Stitch between the large and small dots. Clip the front to the large dot, taking care not to cut any stitches, and grade the seam.

5 STITCH THE NECK EDGE AND MAKE THE DARTS

Tack the dart on each front. Then, with right sides together, pin the rest of the under collar to the jacket, matching the notches. Stitch from the centre back along the stitching line to the point of one dart. Return to the centre back and stitch along the stitching line to the point of the other dart.

6 PREPARE THE JACKET FACING

Make a line of stay stitches along the neck edge of the back facing and between the dots on the lapel edge of the front facings. Stitch the facing sections together at the shoulder seams. Press the seams open. Press 1cm (⅜in) to the wrong side on the inner edges of the front facing and the lower edge of the back facing. Stitch. On the front facing, clip the front facing at the large dot and small dot, being careful not to cut into the stay stitching.

7 STITCH THE UPPER COLLAR TO THE FACING

With right sides together, pin the upper collar to the neck edge of the facing, matching the large and small dots and matching the remaining small dots to the shoulder seams. Stitch between the large dots and layer the seams. Press the seams open.

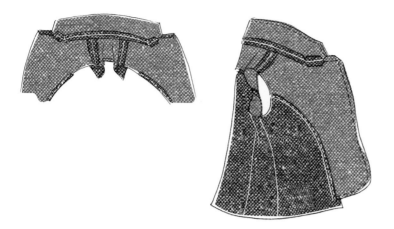

8 STITCH THE UPPER COLLAR AND FACING TO THE JACKET

With right sides together, pin the upper collar and facing to the under collar and jacket, matching the centre back and the large and small dots. You will need to 'ease' the upper collar and facing to fit by pulling it into place as you go and break the stitch at the large dot. Tack and stitch. Grade the seam.

9 FINISH THE HEM AND BODY

Turn the facing to the inside and press. You'll find as you do this, the hem will turn up to the correct length where the facing is sewn onto the front of the jacket. Press the hem up at this level and press in the raw edge by 1.5cm (⅝in) and hand stitch the hem. Lift up the back facing and slipstitch the neck seam allowances together.

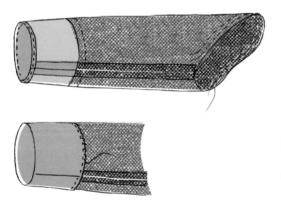

10 PREPARE THE SLEEVES

Run gathering stitches along the sleeve head between the notches. With right sides together, stitch the sleeve seam. Press the seam open. With right sides together, stitch the sleeve facing seams, to form tubes. Press the seams open. With right sides together, pin the raw edge of the facing to the lower edge of the sleeve, matching the seams. Tack and stitch. Press the seam away from the sleeve. On the sleeve facing, press a 1cm (⅜in) hem to the wrong side and stitch. Press the facing to the inside of the sleeve and hand stitch the top edge in place.

11 SET IN THE SLEEVES

Turn the jacket inside out and the sleeve right side out. Put the sleeve into the armhole, matching the small dot with the shoulder seam and matching the underarm seam. Tack the lower part of the sleeve into the armhole position between the notches. At the top of the sleeve, pull up the easing stitches to fit the armhole and distribute the fullness evenly. Tack and stitch. Trim the seam and press the seam allowance to shrink the fullness.

12 ADD THE BUTTONHOLE AND BUTTON

The only finishing touch left is to work the buttonhole on the right front and sew the button on the left front.

*Bow ties don't have to be black or white –
here's your chance to add a splash of colour
to any outfit. This one is made in slubbed
silk, which presses up smartly and comes in
an endless range of colours.*

DIFFICULTY RATING: ⊞ ⊞ ⊞ ⊞ ⊞

Materials

30 x 110cm (12 x 44in) of
    slubbed silk
20 x 90cm (8 x 36in) of
    fine iron-on interfacing
Matching sewing thread
Metal bow-tie hook,
    eye and adjustment
    slider, with 19mm (¾in)
    wide slots

Making a comeback, bow ties are a smart retro accessory.
They really aren't difficult to make and once you've perfected
the techniques to make perfect curves, points and corners, you'll
want to be making them by the dozen for all the boys in your life.
Using very little fabric, they don't cost a lot to make, so they're
also an excellent accessory to make in bulk for school fundraisers.

BOW TIE SIZE
The tie is made in two pieces and the length is adjustable. Each of
the two finished tie pieces measures approximately 7cm (2¾in)
across the widest end and 2cm (¾in) across the narrowest end.

FABRIC FINDER
Bow ties are traditionally made in pure silk, but any fine fabric
that doesn't crease too readily will work as long as it's first backed
with interfacing.
Try these alternatives:
Smooth lightweight silk—Lightweight silk prints—Raw silk—
Fine close-weave cotton

SKILLS SET
Working even slipstitch **see page 48**—Stitching straight seams **see page 51**
Clipping curved seams **see page 52**

Cutting guide

Press the fabric thoroughly and align the threads so warp and weft are as straight as possible before cutting.

FROM THE MAIN FABRIC:

✂ Cut one short tie piece and one long tie piece.

FROM THE MAIN FABRIC WITH INTERFACING:

✂ Iron the interfacing onto the wrong side of the remaining fabric, then cut one short tie piece and one long tie piece.

The 1cm (⅜in) seam allowances are included in the bow tie pieces.

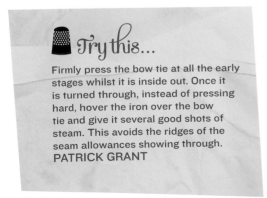

Try this...

Firmly press the bow tie at all the early stages whilst it is inside out. Once it is turned through, instead of pressing hard, hover the iron over the bow tie and give it several good shots of steam. This avoids the ridges of the seam allowances showing through.
PATRICK GRANT

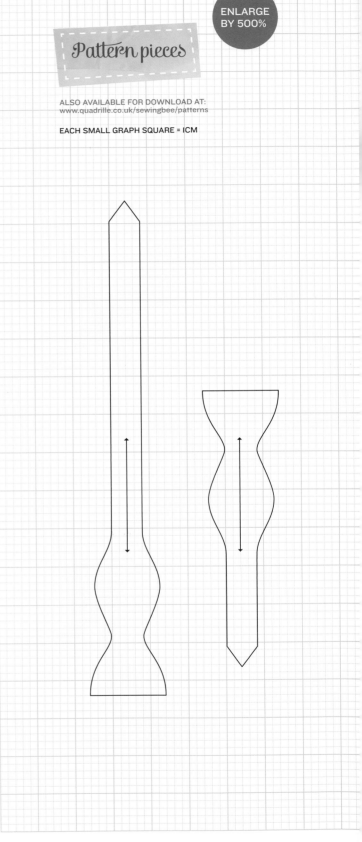

Pattern pieces

ALSO AVAILABLE FOR DOWNLOAD AT:
www.quadrille.co.uk/sewingbee/patterns

EACH SMALL GRAPH SQUARE = ICM

ENLARGE BY 500%

To make the bow tie

1 STITCH THE TIE PIECES TOGETHER
Place the short tie pieces right sides together. Stitch, taking a 1cm (⅜in) seam allowance and leaving an 8cm (3in) gap in the seam along one side of the narrow strip – this is for turning the piece right side out. Keep the 1cm (⅜in) seam width consistent all around the curves, the corners and the point to ensure a neatly shaped tie. Press the seams flat to embed the stitches. Snip off the corners of the seam allowances and clip the curves, taking care not to cut into any of the stitching lines. Stitch and trim the long tie pieces in exactly the same way.

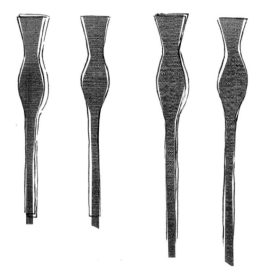

2 COMPLETE THE TWO TIE PIECES
Turn the short and long tie pieces right side out through the gap. Fold in the seam allowances along the gap and slipstitch the sides of the opening together to close it. Press.

3 ADD ON THE TIE HOOK
Thread the narrow pointed end of the short tie piece through the metal bow-tie hook and fold about 4cm (1¼in) of this tie end onto the reverse side of the tie. Slipstitch the pointed end in place.

4 ADD ON THE EYE AND SLIDER
Thread the narrow pointed end of the long tie piece through the slider and then the hook-eye. Now thread the end back around the slider bar in the opposite direction as shown and pin the end down on itself. Slide the slider up and down to check that it works, then slipstitch the pointed end in place.

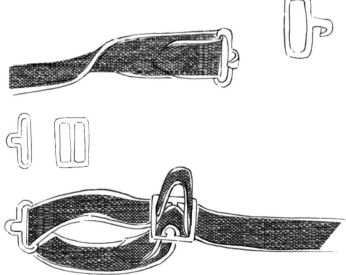

181

To tie the bow tie

5 START TO TIE THE BOW TIE
The tie opens at the back, which means it is kept tied. To tie, first put the bow tie around your neck with the hook and eye at the back and bring the bow parts forwards. Cross the right end over the left and then back up under it.

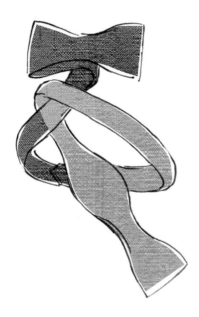

6 START FORMING THE BOW
Fold the left end of the bow tie to the left, then back to the right on top of itself.

7 COMPLETE THE BOW
Bring the right end down over the centre, back up behind it and over to the front again, then fold it in half as you push it through the centre piece. Sounds complicated, but just think of it as tying a neat bow. Take the tie off by unclipping the hook.

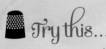 **Try this...**

If you're new to machine stitching, or would like to perfect your skills, make a 'test' bow tie using fabric from your scrap bag. You can leave out the interfacing on this first go.

CAMISOLE

A pretty camisole is a useful wardrobe basic. Team it with a skirt for evening, or give it a daytime look with a pair of jeans. By making your own, you can add quality details like pearl buttons and lace edging.

DIFFICULTY RATING: ⊞ ⊞ ⊞ ⊞ ⊞

Materials

1.5m (1¾yd) of 115cm-
(45in-) wide silk crepe
de Chine or other pure
or fine synthetic silk
Matching sewing thread
Three 1cm (³⁄₈in) mother-
of-pearl buttons
1.3m (1½yd) of lace edging,
about 1.5cm (⁵⁄₈in) wide,
to trim the hem

The delightful pintucked detail on this pretty shell-pink satin camisole is surprisingly easy to achieve. Stitched on a square of satin, it is then cut to shape and stitched onto the main front piece before making up. Real silk satin garments like this are expensive to buy, yet easy to sew, and so are well worth making up at home.

CAMISOLE SIZES
To fit UK women's sizes 8, 10, 12, 14 and 16.

FABRIC FINDER
Pure silk is wonderful against the skin. It's cool in summer, yet provides surprising warmth in the winter when teamed with heavier daywear. Soft ballet-shoe pink is a romantic choice that works well with most other colours.
Try these alternatives:
Silk crepe de Chine—Synthetic silk—Synthetic crepe de Chine—Fine cotton lawn

SKILLS SET
Slipstitching double-fold hems see page 50—Stitching straight seams see page 51
Stitching French seams see page 56—Making and applying bias binding see pages 70 and 71

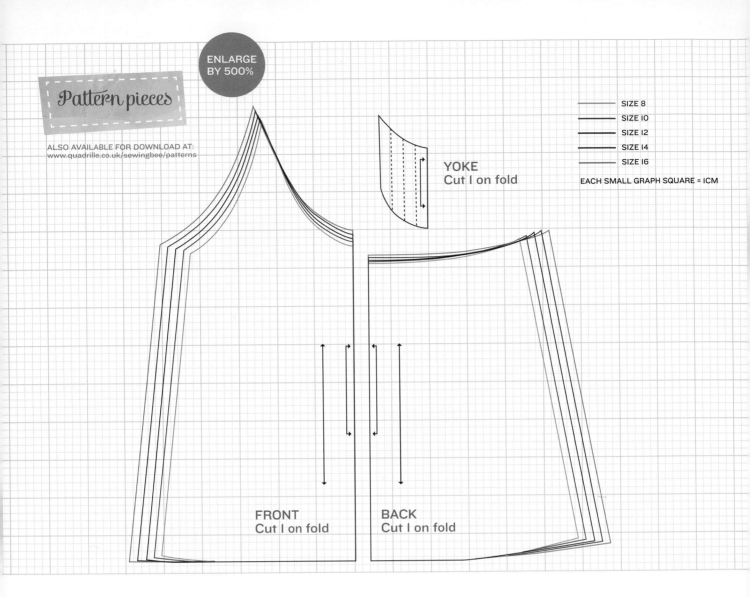

Pattern pieces

ALSO AVAILABLE FOR DOWNLOAD AT:
www.quadrille.co.uk/sewingbee/patterns

YOKE
Cut 1 on fold

SIZE 8
SIZE 10
SIZE 12
SIZE 14
SIZE 16

EACH SMALL GRAPH SQUARE = 1CM

FRONT
Cut 1 on fold

BACK
Cut 1 on fold

Cutting diagram

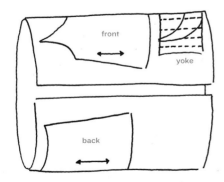

front

yoke

back

Cutting guide

Press the fabric thoroughly before cutting.

FROM THE FABRIC:

✂ Cut one camisole front and one camisole back, both on the fold.

The 1.5cm (⅝in) seam allowances on the side seams and the 12mm (½in) double hem allowances on the hem edges, the top back edge and the front armhole edge are included on all the pattern pieces. The front neck edge does not need a hem allowance as it is bound with a bias strip. Set aside the yoke pattern piece – the yoke is cut out from fabric after it is pintucked. The 6mm (¼in) turn-under on the yoke outside curved edge is added when the piece is cut in step 3. The yoke top edge is bound with a bias strip.

To make the camisole

1 MARK THE PINTUCKS ON THE YOKE
To prepare the pintucked yoke, cut a square of fabric 18 x 18cm (7 x 7in). Using tailor's chalk, mark the positions of the pintucks on the right side of the fabric. Start by drawing two lines 3cm (1¼in) apart at the centre of the fabric, then draw two lines either side of these, each 1.5cm (⅝in) from its neighbour. Alternatively, transfer the pintuck positions from the pattern piece onto the fabric.

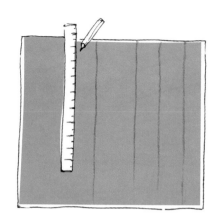

2 STITCH THE PINTUCKS
Fold the fabric along one marked line and, using a zip foot, stitch as close to the fold as you can. Press. Re-fold the fabric on the next line and stitch in the same way. Repeat for all the lines. Press the pintucks away from the centre.

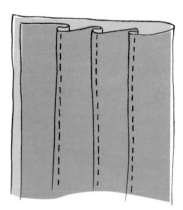

3 CUT OUT THE YOKE SHAPE
With wrong sides together, fold the pintucked fabric along the exact centre between the two centre pintucks. Place the yoke pattern piece on the fold over the prepared pintucks and cut out, adding an extra 6mm (¼in) along the outside curved edge for a turn-under (but not along the neck edge).

4 STITCH ON THE YOKE
Press 6mm (¼in) to the wrong side all around the outside curved edge of the prepared yoke and tack. Position the yoke right side up on top of the right side of the camisole front piece and tack in place. Topstitch around the curved edge, stitching as close as possible to the fold. Remove the tacking. Stitch three buttons to the yoke between the centre pintucks, the first 2.5cm (1in) below the neck edge and the others 2cm (¾in) apart below the first.

5 STITCH THE BACK AND FRONT TOGETHER
Join the side seams using the French seam method. To do this, first place the front piece on the back piece, with wrong sides together, and stitch the side seams 5mm (¼in) from the edge. Press the seams open. Fold along the seamline so the front and back are positioned with right sides together. Stitch again, but this time 1cm (⅜in) from the fold.

6 FINISH THE TOP, ARMHOLE AND HEM EDGES

Stitch double-fold hems along the armhole and top back edges, and along the camisole hemline. For each of these hems, turn under 6mm (¼in) twice, pin and tack. Then stitch close to the first fold of the double-fold hem. (Remember to leave the front neck edge raw, as this will be covered with bias binding.)

7 STITCH ON THE HEM LACE

For a delicate detail, add some lace along the hemline. Starting at one side seam, pin the top edge of the lace edging behind the hemline. Hand sew the ends of the lace together where they meet. Tack the lace in place, then stitch close to the edge of the fabric using a zip foot. Remove the tacking.

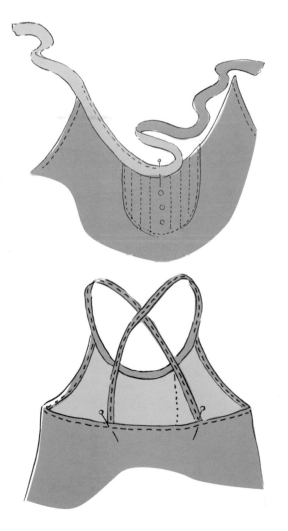

8 CUT THE BIAS BINDING AND BIND THE NECK EDGE

From the fabric, cut enough 2.5cm- (1in-) wide bias strips to piece together a continuous strip 1.5m (1¾yd) long. Make sure your strips are as long as possible and that one is at least 50cm (20in) long. Stitch the pieces together to form the continous strip, using the longest strip at the centre, and press the seams open. Fold the strip in half widthways and mark the centre point. With right sides together, pin this to the centre front of the camisole. Tack from this point to the end of the camisole neck edge. Repeat on the other side. Stitch the binding to the neck edge, starting from the centre in the same way and taking a 6mm (¼in) seam allowance. Press in 6mm (¼in) along the raw edge of the binding where it is stitched to the neck edge, fold to the inside of the camisole and pin. Slipstitch the binding in place along the neck-edge seamline.

9 FINISH THE STRAPS

Turn in and press 6mm (¼in) along both raw edges, then pin together and tack. Using a zip foot, stitch close to the edge. Put the camisole on, bring the straps over your shoulders, cross over and pin to the right length at the back. Stitch in position and trim the ends.

BOYFRIEND SHIRT

A boyfriend shirt is a great off-duty staple that can be worn buttoned up long and loose over leggings or open like a jacket with jeans. Learn to make your own and you'll benefit from endless fabric choices.

DIFFICULTY RATING: ⊞ ⊞ ⊞ ⊞ ⊞

Collars, cuffs, sleeves and button bands all contrive to make shirts something of a challenging project. But this is something of a cheat's shirt so you can achieve the look a little more easily. The yoke is simply applied on top of the main pattern piece – no lining and facing, the sleeves have turn-ups rather than tricky cuffs whilst the buttonhole bands are attached like bias binding.

SHIRT SIZES
To fit UK women's sizes 8, 10, 12, 14 and 16.

FABRIC FINDER
Soft plaid cotton makes a perennial favourite choice for a boyfriend shirt. Easy to handle, the pattern can be cut on the bias for design detail. This basic shirt design can also be made up in pretty prints for a more feminine look.
Try these alternatives:
Brushed plaid cotton—Chambray—Denim—Gabardine—Linen—Printed cotton—Printed cotton lawn

Materials
2.5m (2¾yd) of 140cm- (55in-) wide fabric
Ten 12mm (½in) buttons
Matching sewing thread
Contrasting topstitching thread

SKILLS SET
Working even slipstitch **see page 48**—Slipstitching double-fold hems **see page 50**
Stitching straight seams **see page 51**—Clipping curved seams **see page 52**
Finishing seams **see pages 54 and 55**—Easing **see page 63**
Making and applying bias binding **see pages 70 and 71**—Making buttonholes **see page 72**
Adding buttonholes **see page 73**

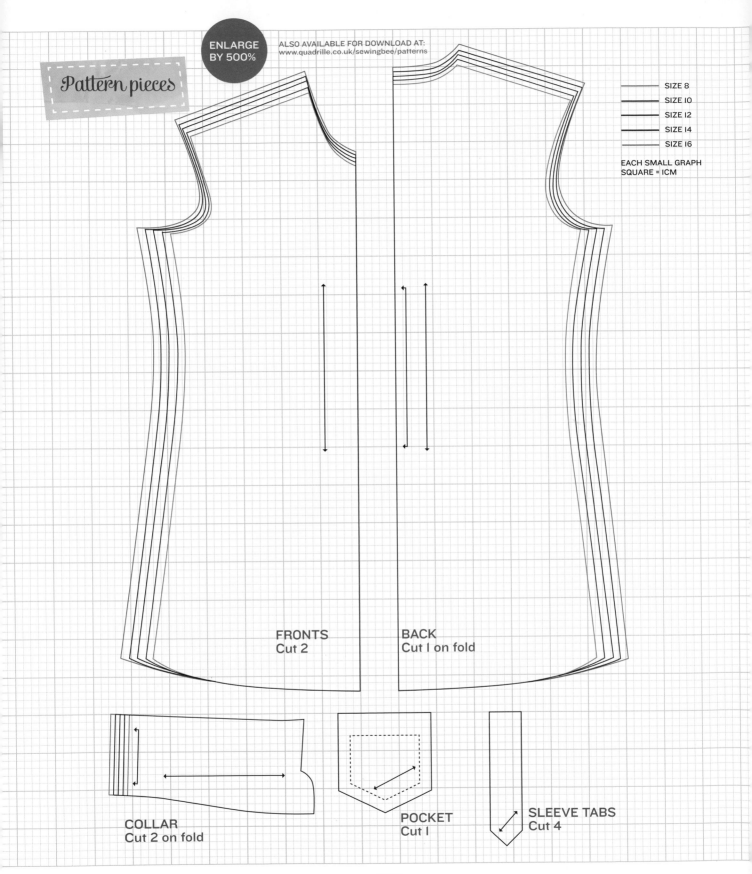

ENLARGE
BY 500%

ALSO AVAILABLE FOR DOWNLOAD AT:
www.quadrille.co.uk/sewingbee/patterns

Pattern pieces

SIZE 8
SIZE 10
SIZE 12
SIZE 14
SIZE 16

EACH SMALL GRAPH
SQUARE = 1CM

FRONTS
Cut 2

BACK
Cut 1 on fold

COLLAR
Cut 2 on fold

POCKET
Cut 1

SLEEVE TABS
Cut 4

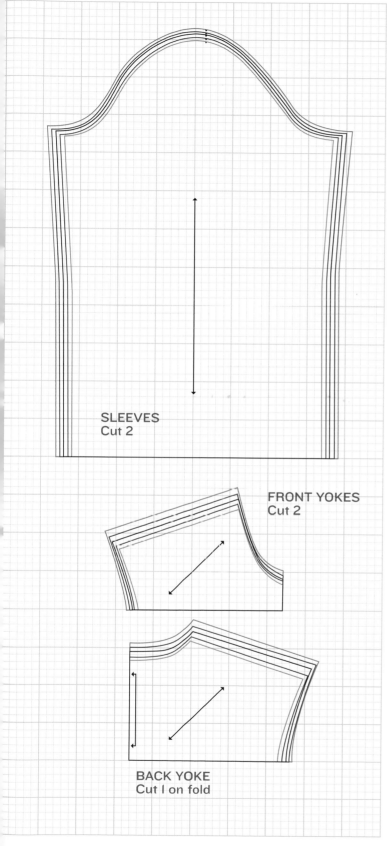

SLEEVES
Cut 2

FRONT YOKES
Cut 2

BACK YOKE
Cut 1 on fold

Cutting diagram

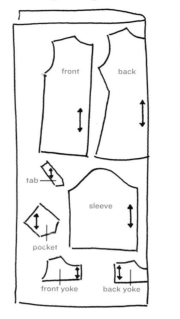

Cutting guide

Press the fabric thoroughly before cutting.

FROM THE FABRIC:

✂ Cut one shirt back, one back yoke and two collar pieces, all on the fold.

✂ Cut two shirt fronts, two shirt sleeves, two front yoke pieces, four sleeve tab pieces and one pocket piece.

The 1cm (⅜in) seam allowances and 3cm (1¼in) shirt and sleeve hem allowances are included on all the pattern pieces. If you want a slightly longer or shorter shirt or sleeves, take this into account when cutting these pieces.

To make the shirt

1 STITCH ON THE YOKE

Press a 1cm (⅜in) hem to the wrong sides at the straight bottom edge of all three yoke pieces. Lay the shirt back right side up and lay the back yoke right side up on top of it, aligning the neck and armhole edges. Tack in position. Topstitch along the folded edge of the yoke, 3mm (⅛in) from the fold. Stitch the front yokes to the shirt fronts in the same way. Remove the tacking.

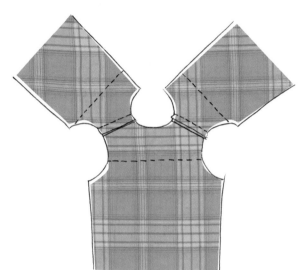

2 STITCH THE SHOULDER SEAMS

With right sides of the back and fronts together and the raw edges aligned, stitch the shoulder seams, taking a 1cm (⅜in) seam allowance. Press the seams open and finish the raw seam edges with zigzag or overlocking stitches if desired.

3 ADD THE FRONT BANDS

Cut a bias strip 8cm (3in) wide and 1.5m (1¾yd) long, piecing strips together as necessary to obtain this length. Fold the strip in half lengthways with right sides together and press. Open up the fold and press 2cm (¾in) to the wrong side along both long edges. Fold the strip in half along the centre again to form the bias binding. Using half of this bias binding for a band along each centre front edge, bind each front edge with this bias binding. Tack, then topstitch them in place. Remove the tacking.

Try this…

If you're worried about working buttonholes neatly, use jeans-style press studs instead, which are no sew and come with a special punch tool.
PATRICK GRANT

4 PREPARE THE POCKET

Press 1.5cm (⅝in) to the wrong side along all sides except the top edge. Tack these hems in place and topstitch 6mm (¼in) from the fold. Remove the tacking. Then press 1.5cm (⅝in) to the wrong side twice along the top edge to form a double hem. Topstitch 1cm (⅜in) from the top edge of the pocket.

5 STITCH ON THE POCKET

Position the pocket on the left front 5cm (2in) below the yoke and 4.5cm (1¾in) from the front band. Using a zip foot, topstitch as close to the edge as you can around the sides and bottom edges.

6 PREPARE THE COLLAR

With right sides together, pin the collar pieces together. Stitch, taking a 1cm (⅜in) seam allowance and leaving the neck edge open. Clip the corners, trim the seam and press it open. Turn the collar right side out and press, positioning the seamline exactly on the fold.

7 STITCH THE COLLAR TO THE SHIRT

With raw edges aligned, pin the collar to the right side of the shirt, matching the ends of the collar with the edge of the front bands. Tack the facing layer to the shirt neckline. Stitch, taking a 1cm (⅜in) seam allowance. Trim the seam and clip the curves. Press open. Turn and press the seam allowance of the collar to the inside. Pin it over the line of stitches along the inside of the neck. Using a zip foot, topstitch as close to the edge as you can. Press. Lastly, topstitch along the outside edge of the collar, 6mm (¼in) from the edge.

8 PREPARE THE SLEEVES

Place two sleeve tabs right sides together, matching the end points. Taking a 1cm (⅜in) seam allowance, stitch along the long edges and the pointed end, leaving the straight end open. Clip the corners, trim the seams, press and turn right side out. Press again. Turn in the open end and slipstitch to close. Topstitch all around the tab 3mm (⅛in) from the edge. Machine stitch a buttonhole at the pointed end of the tab, using topstitching thread. Position the straight end of the tab on the wrong side of the sleeve, about 34cm (13½in) below the top of the sleeve. Stitch in position by sewing a square at the end of the tab and then a cross for security. In the same way, prepare the tab for the other sleeve and stitch it into position. Run easing stitches along the top of both sleeves.

9 STITCH ON THE SLEEVES

With right sides together, pin the sleeve to the armhole, matching the markers to the shoulder seam. Pull up the easing threads and even out the gathers. Stitch, taking a 1cm (⅜in) seam allowance. Repeat with the other sleeve. Trim the seams and clip the curves. Press the seams open and then towards the sleeve. Finish the seam edges.

10 STITCH THE SIDE SEAMS

With right sides together, stitch the side seams, taking a 1cm (⅜in) seam allowance. To do this, start at the hem, work up the side of the shirt to the armhole, and then carry on to stitch down the length of the sleeve. Trim the seams, press them open and then towards the back of the shirt. Finish the raw seam edges. Finally, topstitch along the full length of the seam through all layers, stitching 6mm (¼in) from the seamline and catching in the seam allowance on the wrong side.

11 HEM THE SHIRT AND SLEEVES

Press 1.5cm (⅝in) to the wrong side twice along the end of one sleeve to form a double hem. Topstitch close to the first fold. Repeat on the other sleeve and at the bottom edge of the shirt. Press.

12 MAKE THE BUTTONHOLES

Mark the positions for eight buttonholes on the right front – the first buttonhole is horizontal and is positioned at the end of the collar, the remaining seven buttonholes are vertical and are centred on the right front band. Machine stitch these buttonholes, using topstitching thread. Stitch buttons in position on the left front band. Stitch one button to the right side of each sleeve over the square of stitching joining the tab to the sleeve on the inside. Fold up the sleeve and button the end of the tab onto the sleeve button.

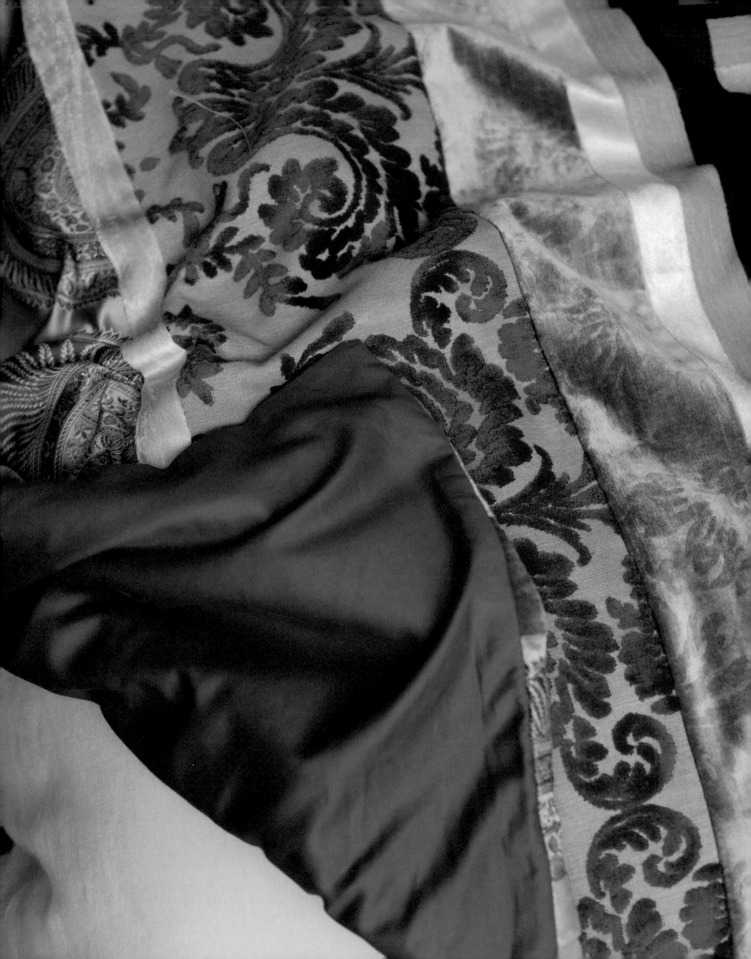

PATCHWORK THROW

This stunning patchwork throw is probably the easiest project in the book. It's just a matter of stitching the strips of upholstery fabric together and backing them with a lining fabric.

DIFFICULTY RATING:

This simple patchwork throw is made up of large strips that are quick and easy to piece together, designed to give you a taster of what may become an absorbing hobby. A centuries-old skill, the most beautiful and intricate patchworks are made up of tiny pieces (traditionally the good bits cut from worn clothes) exactingly pieced together to particular designs with evocative names like Log Cabin, Bear's Paw and Virginia Star. This throw incorporates the general patchwork principles, but is made up of large pieces to create a throw for an armchair or sofa, or even a bed dressing. You can use the principles to make a throw any size simply by using more strips and cutting them longer.

THROW SIZE
The finished throw measures approximately 118cm x 160cm (46½in x 63in). For a bigger throw, see Fabric Finder.

FABRIC FINDER
This throw is made up of sumptuous, tactile furnishing fabrics in silk, velvets and velour, but following craft traditions you can make the patchwork top in any fabric you like. The key is to choose fabrics that are all the same weight.
Try these alternatives:
Cotton shirting—Synthetic velvets—Printed cotton—Satins and sateens—Soft washed cotton—Silk—Washed silk

Materials
60cm (⅔yd) each of two different upholstery-weight fabrics (fabrics A and B), both at least 122cm (48in) wide

50cm (½yd) each of two more upholstery-weight fabrics (fabrics C and D), both at least 122cm (48in) wide

1.7m (2yd) of a solid-coloured curtain-lining fabric, same width as strip fabrics

Sewing thread in a neutral shade that works well with all the fabrics

SKILLS SET
Working even slipstitch **see page 48**—Stitching straight seams **see page 51**

199

Cutting guide

For this throw, the 12 strips of varying depths were cut from fabric 122cm (48in) wide, which makes up the finished width. You can make a wider throw by using fabrics 150cm (60in) wide. Alternatively, piece together two or more strips to make up any preferred width – cut the strips so that the joins don't all fall in the same place. When calculating your strip widths, allow for seam allowances of 1.5cm (⅝in) all round each strip.

FROM FABRIC A:
✂ Cut three strips – one 9.5cm (3¾in) wide, one 18.5cm (7½in) wide and one 24.5cm (9¾in) wide.

FROM FABRIC B:
✂ Cut three strips – one 16cm (6¼in) wide, one 20cm (8in) wide and one 24cm (9½in) wide.

FROM FABRIC C:
✂ Cut three strips – one 9cm (3½in) wide, one 12.5cm (5in) wide and one 20.5cm (8¼in) wide.

FROM FABRIC D:
✂ Cut three strips – one 9.5cm (3¾in) wide, one 12cm (4¾in) wide and one 20cm (8in) wide.

To make the patchwork throw

1 CUT THE STRIPS
Using the cutting guide, cut a total of 12 strips, from selvedge to selvedge. To match the featured throw, follow the given widths.

2 STITCH THE STRIPS TOGETHER IN PAIRS
Work out the best composition by laying out the strips right side up, side by side and with the long edges touching, rearranging them until you are happy with their arrangement. With right sides together, pin the strips together in pairs along the long edges. Stitch together the first pair of strips. Repeat with all the other strips, so you end up with six pairs. Press the seams open.

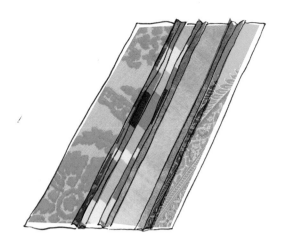

3 STITCH THE PAIRS OF STRIPS TOGETHER

Now stitch the pairs together as precisely as possible, so you have three sets of four strips. Press the seams open as you work for perfectly flat pieces.

4 STITCH THE SETS OF STRIPS TOGETHER

Next stitch the three sets of strips together. Press the remaining seams open. Now press the wrong side of the patchwork top using a hot iron and lots of steam. Work in parallel with the seams. Repeat on the right side. For fabrics with a deep pile, don't apply pressure behind the iron as this will flatten the pile. Instead, hover the iron over the fabric and use plenty of shots of steam. To neaten the raw edges, mark a line close to the edge of each side at right angles to the seam lines using tailor's chalk and a steel edge. Use sharp dressmaker's shears to trim down this line.

5 COMPLETE THE THROW TOP

Lay the lining right side up on a flat surface and lay the patchwork top right side down on top of it. Smooth out the layers and pin them together around the outer edge of the top. Trim the lining to the same size as the patchwork. Stitch the top to the lining around the edge, leaving a 30cm (12in) opening in the seam along one of the short sides. Press the seams flat to embed the stitches and also press the seam allowance back around the 30cm (12in) opening. Clip off the corners of the seam allowances, taking care not to cut too close to the stitching.

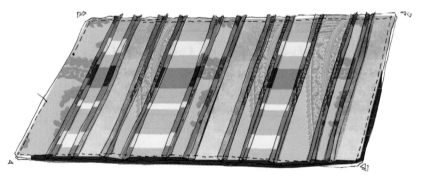

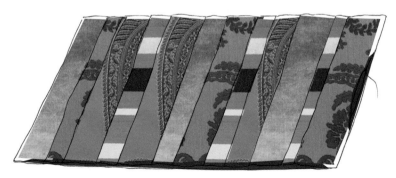

6 HAND SEW THE OPENING

Turn the throw right side out through the opening. Then use a knitting needle (as it has a blunt point) to ease out the corners. Hand stitch the opening using even slipstitch to close it. Finally, press the whole throw flat so the seam lies exactly on the edge for a professional finish.

ROMAN BLIND

Smart and architectural, Roman blinds are a classic window covering. They use a fraction of the fabric needed for curtains, so can be cost-effective. It does take some time to work out the mathematical calculations.

DIFFICULTY RATING: ⊞ ⊞ ⊞ ⊞ ⊡

Materials

Blind fabric in the required amount

Lining fabric in the required amount

Matching sewing thread

2cm- (¾in-) wide Velcro tape, and as long as width of finished blind

12mm (½in) plastic blind-rings, 3 per dowel

Metal cleat, to wrap cords around when blind is up

2.5cm (1in) D-lath, 1cm (½in) shorter than width of finished blind

9mm (⅜in) wooden dowels, each same length as lath and one for about every 30cm (12in) of blind

2.5 x 2.5cm (1 x 1in) support batten, 5mm (¼in) shorter than width of finished blind

Staple gun

4 metal screw eyes

3 nylon blind cords, each twice length of finished blind plus width of blind

Blind pull

Being able to make your own Roman blinds gives you endless fabric choices and can save you a small fortune. They've been given a four button rating because you need something of a mathematician's head to work out the positions of the dowel channels, but once you have, making up the blind requires nothing more than stitching in a straight line. The extra skills that are essential, however, are meticulous measuring and a steady hand on the scissors.

ROMAN BLIND SIZE
The finished Roman blind can be up to 120cm (47in) wide and the desired length. (If you want a wider blind, use more cords and make the blind in a similar fashion.)

FABRIC FINDER
Almost any furnishing or upholstery fabric will work for blinds designed to cut out light. There's no reason why you shouldn't make a sheer version in crisp organdie, for example. However, as you'd be able to see through the blind to the cords, you may want to substitute organza ribbons for operating the blind.
Try these alternatives:
Cottons—Cotton mixes—Linen—Linen union—Furnishing synthetics

SKILLS SET
Working even slipstitch **see page 48**
Stitching straight seams **see page 51**

202

Measuring guide

**FOR THE FINISHED
BLIND WIDTH:**
Decide whether you want the blind to fit inside the window recess or across it and measure this width – this is the finished blind width.

**FOR THE FINISHED
BLIND LENGTH:**
Decide the position of batten support at top of window, then measure from the top of the batten to where the bottom of blind should reach – this is the finished blind length.

Cutting guide

FROM THE BLIND FABRIC:
✎ Cut a panel of fabric that is as wide as the desired finished blind width plus 8cm (3in) extra, and as long as the desired finished blind length plus 13cm (5in) extra.

FROM THE LINING FABRIC:
✎ Cut a panel of fabric that is 1cm (½in) narrower than the blind fabric panel. The length of the lining panel is the finished blind length, plus 4cm (1½in) extra for each horizontal dowel channel. (This means that once the channels are folded and stitched, the lining is the exact length of the finished blind.) You will need one dowel channel every 30cm (12in), starting from the top of the blind; below the last dowel channel there should be 15cm (6in) to the bottom edge of the blind. The distance between the channels can be a little more, or less, but make the distance to the hem below the last channel, half of the distance between the dowels. To calculate how many dowel channels you need, draw the finished blind measurements to scale on graph paper and then draw lines across it at the position of each dowel – make sure the dowel channels are equally spaced.

To make the blind

1 CUT OUT THE BLIND AND LINING PANELS
Follow the measuring and cutting guides, cut out the blind and lining panels. Be sure to make a graph-paper scale drawing of the dowel positions on your blind as suggested – and keep it safe.

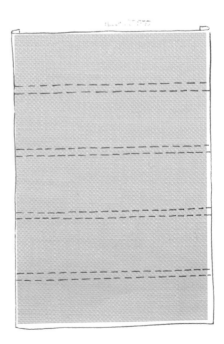

2 MARK THE DOWEL-CHANNEL POSITIONS
First, prepare the lining. Press 4cm (1½in) to the wrong side along each side edge of the lining panel and tack in place. Now mark the dowel-channel positions across the right side of the lining. This must be done accurately so take your time. Referring to your scale drawing and using a retractable pencil, draw the first horizontal line the distance from the top of the lining as the first marked channel position. Draw a line 4cm (1½in) below this – this is the first channel. Draw the remaining channel positions in exactly the same way – with two lines 4cm (1½in) apart.

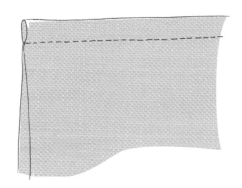

3 MACHINE STITCH THE DOWEL CHANNELS
With wrong sides together, fold the lining along the centre of the first dowel channel, so the two marked lines are aligned, press well along this fold and then pin. Stitch 2cm (¾in) from the pressed fold (along the marked line). Stitch the remaining channels in the same way.

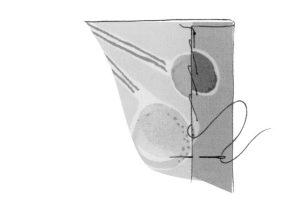

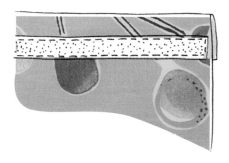

4 PREPARE THE BLIND FABRIC
Press 4cm (1½in) to the wrong side along each side edge of the blind panel and pin in place. Then sew these hems in place along the raw edge, using a catch stitch that will be almost invisible on the right side of the blind. Next, at the bottom of the blind fabric, press 1cm (½in), then 4cm (1½in) to the wrong side. At the top of the blind fabric, press 4cm (1½in) to the wrong side twice. These pressed folds now indicate the positions for the top and bottom hems – do not pin or tack these hems yet. Now unfold the second fold of the double hem at the top of the blind, so only the first 4cm (1½in) is folded to the wrong side. Pin the soft section of the Velcro tape to the right side of the blind fabric, just above the second pressed foldline so it sits on the double layer of fabric. Stitch the Velcro in place all around its edge.

5 SLIPSTITCH THE LINING TO THE BLIND PANEL
With the top and bottom blind hems unfolded and with wrong sides together, lay the lining fabric on top of the blind fabric. Position the lining so its top edge is aligned with the hemline fold at the top and the bottom edge is aligned with the hemline fold at the bottom. Then centre the lining widthways on the blind fabric, so there is 5mm (¼in) more blind fabric along each side edge. Pin and slipstitch the sides of the lining to the blind fabric between the dowel channels.

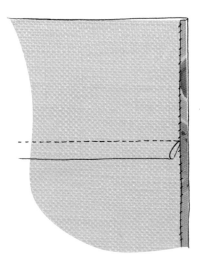

6 SLIPSTITCH THE TOP AND BOTTOM HEMS
Fold the pressed hems at the top and bottom of the blind over
the lining and pin. Slipstitch the top and bottom hems in place. At
the top of the blind, slipstitch the sides of the hem together. Leave
the sides of the hem at the bottom open, for inserting the lath.

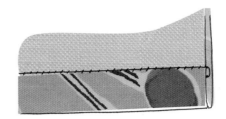

7 SEW ON THE RINGS
Measure and, using a pencil, mark three ring positions on
each dowel channel. The cords will be threaded through these
rings to pull up the blind. Mark one ring position in the exact
centre of the channel and one 4.5cm (1¾in) from each end. Hand
sew a ring at each of these positions, catching in the pressed
channel fold.

8 INSERT THE DOWELS AND THE LATH
Slip one dowel into each channel and slipstitch the ends to
close. Slide the D-lath into the hem channel at the bottom of the
blind and slipstitch the ends to close.

9 PREPARE THE BATTEN SUPPORT
Staple the hook section of the Velcro tape to the front of the
batten. Screw the three screw eyes to the bottom of the batten,
one 5cm (2in) from each end and one at the centre. Add an extra
screw eye 2.5cm (1in) from the pull-cord end. Fix a cleat to the
architrave on the same side. Fix the batten to the window.

10 THREAD ON THE BLIND CORDS
Knot one end of each cord onto one of the
three rings at the bottom of the blind. Feed each
cord up through the other rings to the top of
the blind. Stick the blind to the batten and then
thread the cords through the screw eyes on the
batten and out at the pull-cord side. With the
blind down, align the cords and attach the blind
pull to the ends, trimming the cords to the same
length. Pull up the blind with the joined cord and
secure on the cleat.

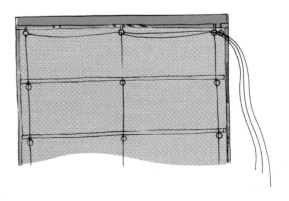

Try this...

To dress up the blind support batten, paint it the colour of the blind or cover it by stapling a lightweight fabric over it.

BASIC DRESS

This simple dress is amazingly versatile. Made here in a lightweight plaid, it has a classic look and can be worn in the winter as a tunic over a blouse. Make it in black velvet and you have a Little Black Dress for the evening or try it in cotton for everyday wear.

DIFFICULTY RATING: ⬤ ⬤ ⬤ ⬤ ⬤

If you only want to learn to make one dress, then this is the one you need to tackle. It's an LBD – Little Basic Dress. It could be black, of course, but then it needn't be. You can choose the colour, the print and the fibre content without being limited by what happens to be in the shops this season. The reason this is the most useful dress to learn to sew is that it is almost a dressmaking sampler, incorporating most of the basic skills: darts, facings and a zip. Best of all, it doesn't use much fabric and it doesn't take long to sew.

Materials
1.6m (1¾yd) of 140cm- (55in-) wide soft lightweight dress fabric
Matching invisible zip, 43cm (17in) long
Matching sewing thread

DRESS SIZES
To fit UK women's sizes 8, 10, 12, 14 and 16.

FABRIC FINDER
This dress is made up in lightweight mixed fibre plaid for an all season garment. Worn with a shirt and/or cardigan, it would also make a fun summer dress on its own. As a basic dress, however, most dress fabrics would work.
Try these alternatives:
Printed cotton—Linen—Cotton mixes—Linen mixes—Denim—Chambray—Velvet—Velour—Devore—Jacquard—Lightweight wool and wool blends—Mixed fibre crepe—Shantung

SKILLS SET
Working even slipstitch see page 48—Stitching straight seams see page 51
Slipstitching double-fold hems see page 50—Clipping curved seams see page 52
Finishing seams see pages 54 and 55—Stitching darts see pages 60 and 61
Inserting an invisible zip see pages 68 and 69

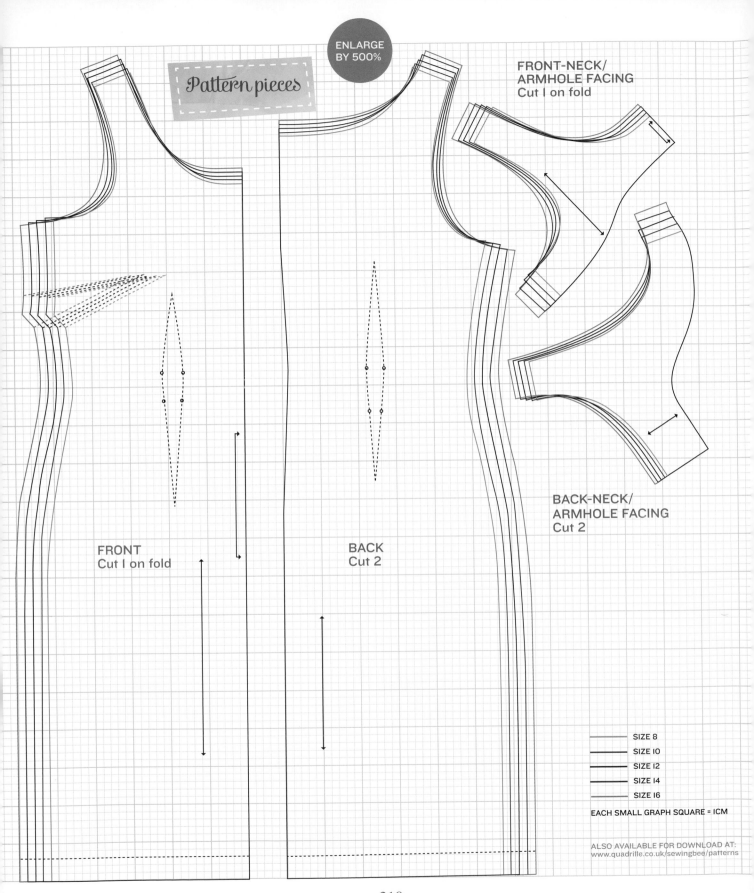

ENLARGE
BY 500%

Pattern pieces

FRONT-NECK/
ARMHOLE FACING
Cut 1 on fold

BACK-NECK/
ARMHOLE FACING
Cut 2

FRONT
Cut 1 on fold

BACK
Cut 2

SIZE 8
SIZE 10
SIZE 12
SIZE 14
SIZE 16

EACH SMALL GRAPH SQUARE = 1CM

ALSO AVAILABLE FOR DOWNLOAD AT:
www.quadrille.co.uk/sewingbee/patterns

210

Cutting diagram

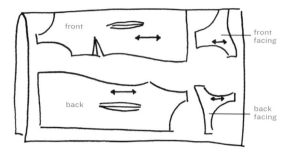

front
front facing
back
back facing

Cutting guide

Press the fabric thoroughly before cutting.

FROM THE FABRIC:

✂ Cut one dress front and one front-neck/armhole facing, both on the fold.

✂ Cut two dress backs and two back-neck/armhole facings.

The 1cm (⅜in) seam allowances and 3cm (1¼in) hem allowances are included on all the pattern pieces.

To make the dress

1 STITCH THE DARTS

Mark and stitch the darts on the dress front and both back pieces. Press the waist darts towards the centre of the dress and the bust darts downwards.

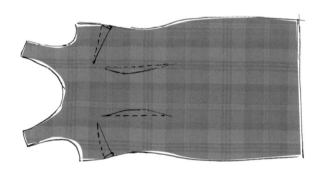

2 INSERT THE ZIP

Insert an invisible zip between the two back pieces and stitch the lower part of the seam, taking a 1cm (⅜in) seam allowance. Press the seam open. Finish the raw edges of the seam with zigzag or overlocking stitches.

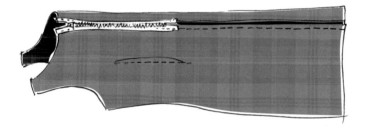

3 STITCH THE BACK AND FRONT TOGETHER

With the right sides of the back and front together, stitch the side seams, taking 1cm (⅜in) seam allowances. Press the seams open. Finish the raw edges of the seam with zigzag or overlocking stitches. Leave the shoulder seams unstitched.

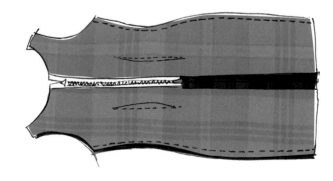

4 PREPARE THE FACING

With right sides together, pin, stitch the side seams of the all-in-one neck/armhole facing. Press the seams open. Finish the bottom raw edge of the facing with zigzag or overlocking stitches. As on the dress, leave the shoulder seams unstitched.

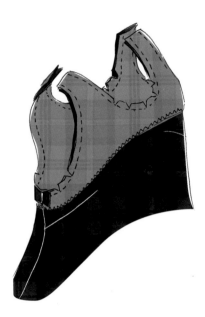

5 STITCH ON THE FACING

With right sides together, pin the facing to the dress, matching the side seams and aligning the neck and armhole edges. Pin and tack around the neckline and the armholes. Stitch, taking 1cm (⅜in) seam allowances. Remove the tacking. Trim the seams and clip the curves. Press the seams open.

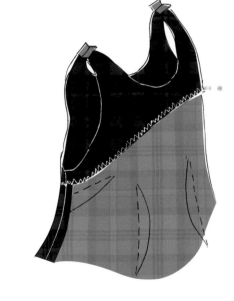

6 STITCH THE SHOULDER SEAMS

Turn the facing to the inside of the dress and press. With the right sides of the dress together, stitch the shoulder seams, stitching through both the dress and facing and using a 1cm (⅜in) seam allowance. Press the seams open and slipstitch the seam allowances to the dress along the outer edges. Turn in the ends of the facing near the zip and slipstitch to the zip tape close to the zip.

7 STITCH THE HEM

Press 5mm (¼in) to the wrong side along the hemline, then press 2.5cm (1in) to the wrong side to form a double-fold hem. Machine stitch the hem in place, stitching close to the first fold.

WAISTCOAT

*A simple waistcoat is surprisingly easy
and hugely satisfying to make because
once the lining is attached and it is turned
right side out, all the seams are enclosed
for an incredibly professional finish.*

DIFFICULTY RATING:

Materials

90cm (1yd) of wool twill
    at least 140cm (55in)
    wide, for main fabric
90cm (1yd) of contrasting
    wool twill at least 140cm
    (55in) wide, for lining
    fabric
Two 2cm (¾in) button
    moulds for covered
    buttons, or two 2cm
    (¾in) buttons
Matching sewing thread

This one is designed for a man, but any waistcoat is made using the same basic method. Endlessly versatile, the waistcoat is the ultimate layering garment, especially in a woman's wardrobe. It can be used to smarten up any combination or perversely, bring a touch of the casual. A fashion favourite for a surprisingly long time, the waistcoat has an illustrious past dating back to the seventeenth century. Originally from Persia, one of Charles II's returning ambassadors introduced the waistcoat to the English court and it soon became de rigueur for English nobility.

WAISTCOAT SIZES
To fit UK men's sizes S, M, L, XL and XXL.

FABRIC FINDER
This waistcoat has been made and fully lined in two shades of fine wool twill, which is a perfect choice for a traditional man's waistcoat. Men's waistcoats are generally made from suitings, wools or brocades whilst women's can be made in almost any dress fabric or suiting.
Try these alternatives:
Heavyweight cotton—Heavyweight linen—Denim—Silk brocade—
Silk-wool mixes—Gabardine—Twill

SKILLS SET
Working even slipstitch **see page 48**—Stitching straight seams **see page 51**
Clipping curved seams **see page 52**— Stitching single-point darts **see page 60**
Making buttonholes **see page 72**

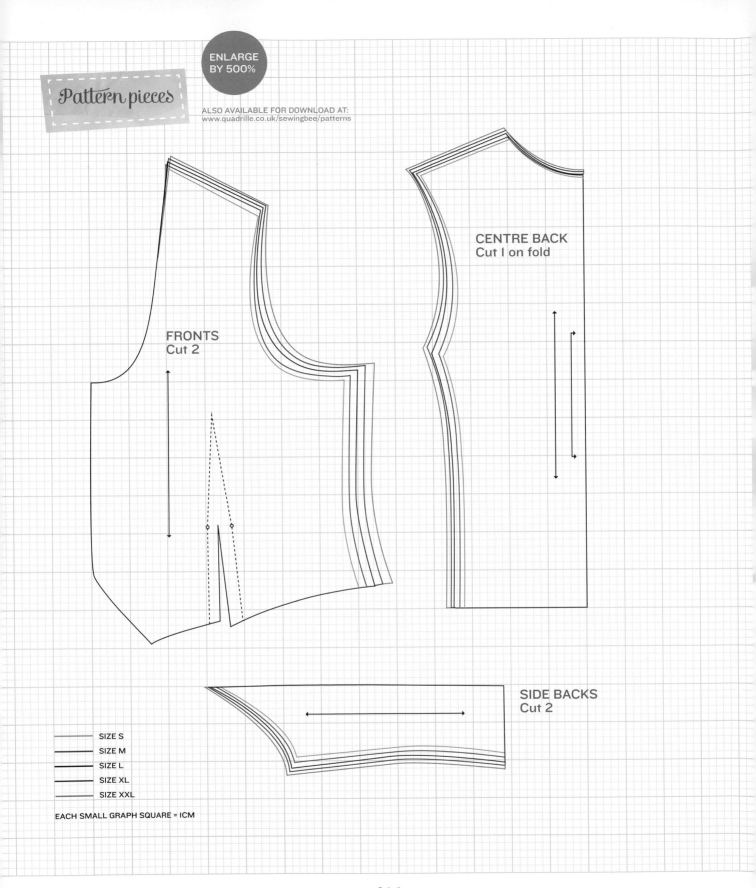

ENLARGE
BY 500%

ALSO AVAILABLE FOR DOWNLOAD AT:
www.quadrille.co.uk/sewingbee/patterns

Pattern pieces

FRONTS
Cut 2

CENTRE BACK
Cut 1 on fold

SIDE BACKS
Cut 2

SIZE S
SIZE M
SIZE L
SIZE XL
SIZE XXL

EACH SMALL GRAPH SQUARE = 1CM

Cutting diagram

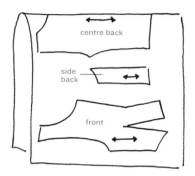

Cutting guide

Press the fabric thoroughly before cutting.

FROM THE MAIN FABRIC:

✂ Cut one centre back on the fold.

✂ Cut two fronts and two side backs.

FROM THE LINING FABRIC:

✂ Cut one centre back on the fold.

✂ Cut two fronts and two side backs.

The 1.5cm (⅝in) seam allowances are included on all the pattern pieces. Be sure to draw around the front dart outline onto the wrong side of the main and lining front pieces with tailor's chalk, to ensure that you can stitch a precise dart shape.

To make the waistcoat

1 STITCH THE DARTS
First, make the outer layer of the waistcoat. Start by stitching the darts on the two main-fabric front pieces. Press the darts towards the centre of the waistcoat.

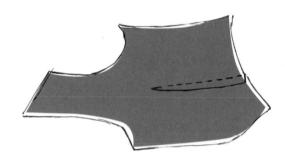

2 STITCH THE BACK PIECES TOGETHER
With right sides together, stitch the main-fabric back side panels to the main-fabric centre-back piece. Trim the seams and press the seams open.

3 STITCH THE SHOULDER SEAMS
With right sides of the fronts and back together, stitch the shoulder seams. Trim the seams and press them open.

4 PREPARE THE LINING
Stitch the darts and all the seams on the lining pieces as for the main-fabric pieces.

5 STITCH ON THE LINING

Lay the outer main-fabric waistcoat right side up on a flat surface and the lining right side down on top of it. Pin and tack along the back hemline; around the armholes; and then along the front hemline, up the front, around the neckline and down the other front side and along its hemline. Stitch. Remove the tacking. Trim the seams, clip the curves and snip off the points, taking care not to cut into any of the stitches. Press the seams open.

6 STITCH THE MAIN-FABRIC SIDE SEAMS

Turn the whole garment right side out – first turn the back right side out through the open side seams, then pull the fronts right side out by pulling them through at the shoulders. Then with right sides together, stitch the side seams of the outer shell (through the open lining side seams). Press the seams open.

7 SLIPSTITCH THE LINING SIDE SEAMS

On the inside of the waistcoat, at one side seam, fold the edge of the back lining piece over the front lining piece and pin. Slipstitch to close. Repeat with the other lining side seam.

8 COVER THE BUTTONS AND MAKE THE BUTTONHOLES

If you are using covered buttons, make two covered buttons, using the contrasting wool twill lining fabric. Mark positions for two horizontal buttonholes on the left front, about 7.5cm (3in) apart and centred on the overlap. Machine stitch one buttonhole in each of the marked positions. Sew the buttons to the right front in corresponding positions.

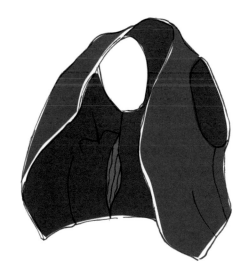

TOTE BAG

A practical tote bag is a very useful accessory. Make yours a one-off original in canvas for the beach or in an upholstery fabric in an interesting print.

DIFFICULTY RATING:

S titch up a smart tote bag to complement your wardrobe. Once you've got the knack, you can stitch up several more – either to suit the changing seasons or make as presents. This tote is designed with suede leather handle details for a super chic finish, though the idea can be easily adapted for cloth handles should you be daunted by the idea of stitching leather.

TOTE BAG SIZE
The finished bag measures 33cm (13in) wide x 28cm (11in) tall, and has a 9.5cm- (3¾in-) wide gusset.

FABRIC FINDER
Tote bags need to be robust, hold their shape and resist the dirt. For this reason, strong, tightly woven fabrics are the best – though be warned, stitching through several layers can be a challenge if you use too heavy a fabric... The lining can always be made in a lighter fabric. If you're daunted by machine stitching leather, make the straps in fabric too.

Try these alternatives for the outer cover:
Any upholstery fabric—Cotton ducks—Light canvas—Denims—
Cotton drill—Gabardine—Ticking
Try these alternative for the lining:
Lightweight printed cottons—Tana lawn—Dress lining (acetate)

Materials
- 50cm (½yd) of a medium-weight fabric print at least 115cm (45in) wide
- 50cm (½yd) of lining fabric at least 115cm (45in) wide
- 50 x 90cm (18 x 36in) of medium-weight iron-on woven interfacing
- 20 x 80cm (8 x 32in) of soft lightweight leather for handles
- Sewing thread to match the bag and lining fabrics, and the strap leather
- Topstitching thread to match both the bag and lining fabrics
- Topstitching thread that contrasts with the strap leather
- 4 metal bag-handle loops with 1.5cm- (⅝in-) wide detachable cross-bars
- Sewing-machine needle (size 80) and leather sewing-machine needle (size 100)

SKILLS SET
Working even slipstitch **see page 48**—Stitching straight seams **see page 51**
Stitching curved seams **see page 52**

221

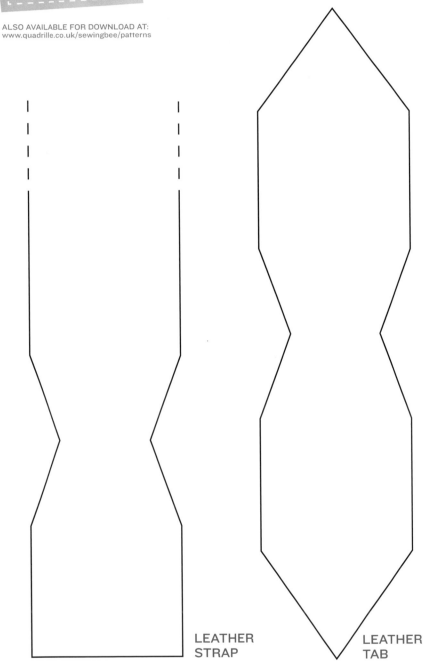

Pattern pieces

LEATHER
STRAP

LEATHER
TAB

Cutting guide

Press the fabrics thoroughly
before cutting.

FROM THE MAIN BAG FABRIC:
✄ Cut one bag front and one
bag back, each 36cm wide x
31cm (14¼in wide x 12¼in).
✄ Cut one bag gusset,
measuring 12.5 x 90cm
(5 x 35½in).

FROM THE LINING FABRIC:
✄ Cut one bag back, front
and gusset the same size as
the bag pieces.

FROM THE STRAP LEATHER:
✄ Cut two straps, each
4 x 79cm (1½ x 31¼in).
✄ Cut four tab pieces,
each 4 x 17cm (1½ x 7in).
The 1.5cm (⅝in) seam
allowances are included on
all the fabric pattern pieces.

To make the tote bag

1 **SHAPE AND TOPSTITCH THE STRAP ENDS**
Take one strap and, using the full-size template given for the leather strap, trace the shape on to the wrong side of the leather. Trim along the outlines. Shape the other ends of the strap in the same way. On each strap end, make a small snip in the leather where indicated – these snips allow the strap to fit neatly on the bag-handle loop. Use a leather needle on the sewing machine and the contrasting topstitching thread on both the bobbin and upper thread, and set the machine to a long stitch length. Stitch together the two layers of each strap end, stitching 3mm (⅛in) from the edge on the two sides and 1cm (½in) from the lower folded edge to allow the metal loop to pass through easily. Begin and end the stitching about 7mm (¼in) past the two layers.

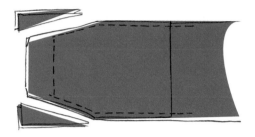

2 **TOPSTITCH ALONG THE LENGTH OF THE STRAP**
Fold the long single-layer part of one strap in half lengthways. Machine topstitch the length of the leather strap between the ends you have already prepared, 3mm (⅛in) from the edge. Be sure to start and end the stitching so it overlaps the strap-end topstitching. Repeat for the other shoulder strap.

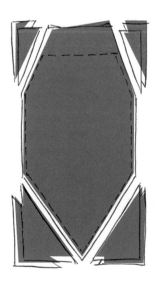

3 **PREPARE THE LEATHER TABS**
Take one leather-tab rectangle and, using the full-size template given for the leather tab, trace the shape on to the wrong side of the leather. Trim along the outlines. Shape the other leather tabs in the same way. Using ordinary thread that matches the leather, topstitch as for the strap ends, stitching 3mm (⅛in) from the edge all around the tab except parallel to the fold where the stitching should be 1cm (½in) from the fold to leave room for the bag-handle cross-bar. Make a little snip into the fold at each side as for the strap end. Prepare the remaining three tabs in the same way.

4 PREPARE THE MAIN BAG PIECES

Iron the interfacing onto the wrong side of the fabric-print front and back. Next, trim the bottom corners of the front and back into gentle curves. (Remember that the top and bottom edges are longer than the bag is tall.) Draw a lightly pencilled gentle curve on the interfaced side on each of the two bottom corners, that is approximately 1.5cm (⅝in) at its farthest from the corner point. Cut along the pencilled lines.

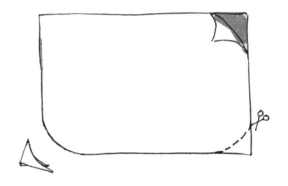

5 STITCH ON THE LEATHER TABS

Place two leather tabs on the bag front, 10cm (4in) down from the top and 5cm (2in) in from each side. Use self-adhesive tape instead of pins to keep them in position. Using the contrasting topstitching thread, stitch around all sides following the first line of topstitching.

6 PREPARE THE LINING PIECES

So that the lining will sit more comfortably inside the bag, trim off 1cm (⅜in) from the bottom edge of the front piece. Then trim a little off both side edges – start at the bottom edge, cutting 5mm (¼in) from the edge and as you near the top edge taper the amount to 3mm (⅛in). Round the bottom corners as for the outer bag. Trim the back piece in the same way so that the front and back are now the same size.

7 STITCH THE LINING PIECES TOGETHER

Using matching thread and a size 80 sewing-machine needle, stitch the lining gusset to the lining front – down one side, along the bottom and up the other side. Now join the back to the gusset, stitching in the same direction for the front seam. Take your time at the corners, sewing and gently easing the gusset fabric around them. Leave a 15cm (6in) opening in one of the seams for turning the bag right side out.

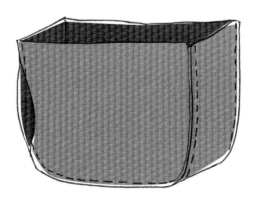

Try this...

If you can only find metal bag-
handle loops that are bigger or
smaller than the ones recommended,
make the strap ends and tabs
wider or narrower at the folds to
accommodate the different size.

8 TOPSTITCH THE LINING SEAMS
Press the lining seam allowances towards the gusset. Then using a matching topstitching thread, topstitch 3mm (⅛in) from each seamline on the gusset side of the seam. Take special care when topstitching around the rounded corners. Topstitching is not just decorative, it provides extra strength as well.

9 SEW THE BAG PIECES TOGETHER
Repeat steps 7 and 8 for the outer shell of the bag, but don't leave an opening in one gusset seam this time. Remember to stitch both gusset seams in the same direction and place the topstitching on the gusset side of the seamlines.

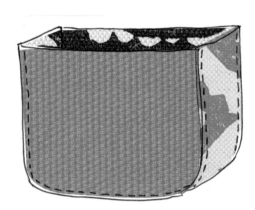 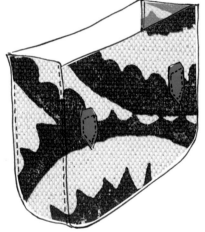

10 STITCH THE LINING TO THE BAG
With right sides together, place the lining inside the outer shell and align the upper raw edges and pin together. Stitch around the top twice for extra strength.

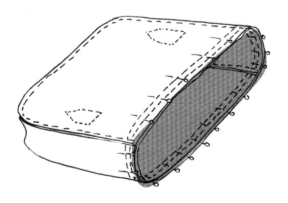

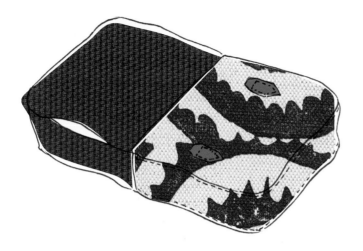

11 TURN THE BAG RIGHT SIDE OUT
Remove the pins and turn the bag right side out through the opening left in the lining seam. Press the seam allowances towards the lining. Slipstitch the opening in the lining seam closed.

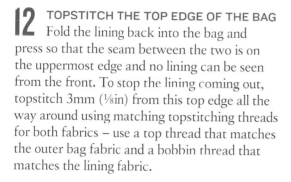

12 TOPSTITCH THE TOP EDGE OF THE BAG
Fold the lining back into the bag and press so that the seam between the two is on the uppermost edge and no lining can be seen from the front. To stop the lining coming out, topstitch 3mm (⅛in) from this top edge all the way around using matching topstitching threads for both fabrics – use a top thread that matches the outer bag fabric and a bobbin thread that matches the lining fabric.

13 ADD THE FINISHING TOUCHES
Fold the bag sides in like a paper bag, so the outer fabric sides are pinched together. Starting at the top edge, topstitch along the fold for about 10cm (4in) through all layers of the bag. This makes the bag 'sit' better for a smarter look. Finally, attach the straps using the detachable metal handle loops, ensuring that the handles lay flat and are not twisting.

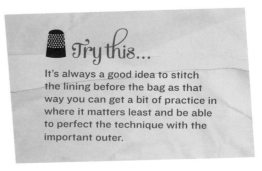

Try this...

It's always a good idea to stitch the lining before the bag as that way you can get a bit of practice in where it matters least and be able to perfect the technique with the important outer.

BLOUSE WITH COLLAR

Gracefully feminine, a simple blouse is the dressmaker's staple. Make it up in delicate silk or chiffon, like this, or choose a more robust plain or printed cotton or linen for effortless elegance.

DIFFICULTY RATING: ⊞ ⊞ ⊞ ⊞ ⊞

Materials

- 1.4m (1½yd) of 115cm- (45in-) wide silk crepe, or 1m (1⅛yd) of 140cm- (55in-) wide silk, for main fabric
- 25cm (¼yd) of a sheer silk print, for collar
- 25cm (¼yd) of cream silk, for collar interlining
- 70cm (¾yd) of contrasting 3mm (⅛in) double-satin ribbon (optional)
- Sewing threads to match main fabric, collar fabric and ribbon

A beautifully stitched blouse is a wonderful addition to a woman's wardrobe. But let's be realistic: collars can be tricky, buttonholes too easily bodged and set-in sleeves a veritable trap for novice stitchers. So here's the solution: the prettiest blouse with no fastenings, a delightful cheat's Peter Pan collar and simple-to-stitch short sleeves. You won't need much fabric, so you can afford to splash out on special materials.

BLOUSE SIZES
To fit UK women's sizes 8, 10, 12, 14 and 16.

FABRIC FINDER
You can totally transform the look of this blouse by using a printed fabric instead of a plain for the main fabric – small-scale prints for a feminine look or large-scale prints for a bold statement. Choosing a matching or contrasting collar is up to you, but use the same weight for both fabrics.
Try these alternatives:
Flowing synthetic silk—Soft fine cottons—Plain lightweight cotton prints—Fine jersey—Lightweight linens

SKILLS SET
Slipstitching double-fold hems **see page 50**—Clipping curved seams **see page 52**
Stitching French seams **see page 56**—Making and applying bias binding **see pages 70 and 71**

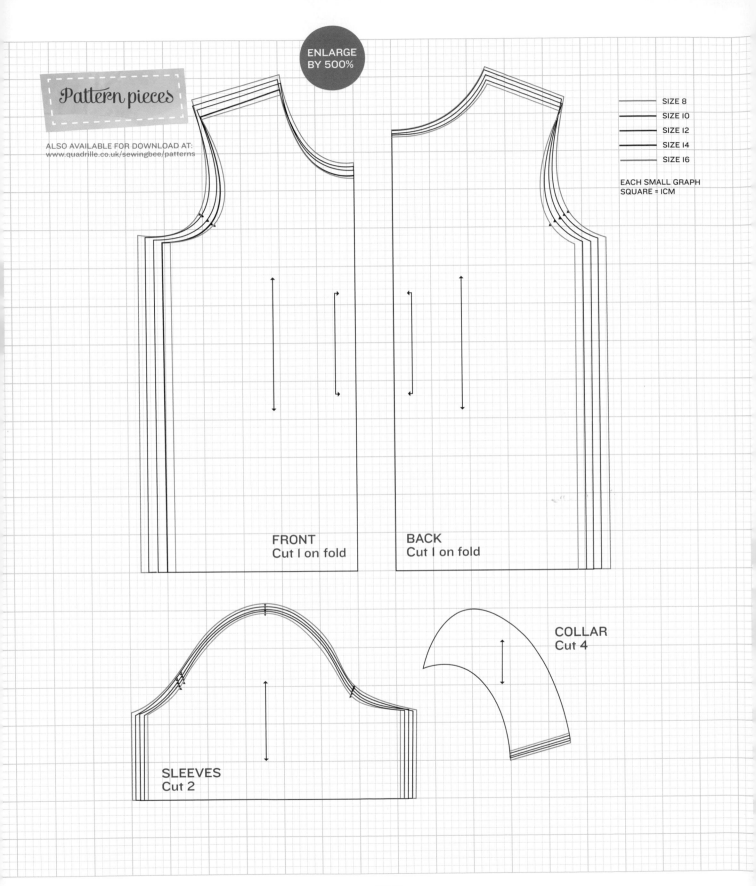

Pattern pieces

ALSO AVAILABLE FOR DOWNLOAD AT:
www.quadrille.co.uk/sewingbee/patterns

ENLARGE
BY 500%

SIZE 8
SIZE 10
SIZE 12
SIZE 14
SIZE 16

EACH SMALL GRAPH
SQUARE = 1CM

FRONT
Cut 1 on fold

BACK
Cut 1 on fold

COLLAR
Cut 4

SLEEVES
Cut 2

230

Cutting diagram

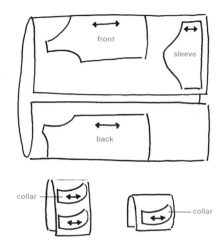

Cutting guide

Press the fabric thoroughly before cutting.

FROM THE MAIN FABRIC:

✎ Cut one front and one back, both on the fold.

✎ Cut two sleeves.

✎ Cut one bias strip 4cm (1½in) wide and 80cm (32in) long.

FROM THE COLLAR FABRIC:

✎ Cut four collars.

FROM THE INTERLINING FABRIC:

✎ Cut two collars.

The 1.5cm (⅝in) seam allowances and 2cm (¾in) hem allowances on the front and back hemline edges and 3cm (1¼in) hem allowances on the sleeve hemline edges are included on all the pattern pieces. Note that you need two collar pieces facing one way and two facing the other way.

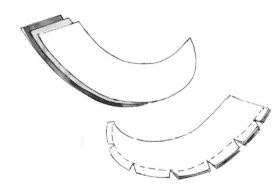

To make the blouse

1 PREPARE THE COLLAR

Place two collar pieces right sides together and place one interlining collar piece on top of this. Tack around the outer curved edge, then stitch. Trim the seam and clip the curves. Remove the tacking and press the seam open. Turn right side out and tack around the curved seam. Prepare the other side of the collar in the same way. Topstitch around the curves close to the edge. Finally, remove the tacking and press.

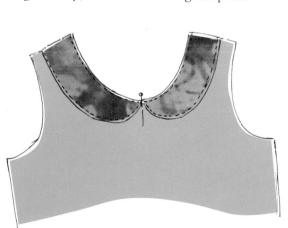

2 TACK THE COLLAR IN PLACE

Fold the blouse front in half and mark the centre of the neckline with a pin. Place the collar pieces on the front, using the marker pin to centre them and aligning them with the raw edges of the neckline and shoulder seams. Tack in position.

3 STITCH THE SHOULDER SEAMS

Using the French seam method, stitch the shoulder seams. To do this, first place the front piece on the back piece, with wrong sides together, and pin along both shoulders. Tack, then stitch each shoulder seam 5mm (¼in) from the edge. Remove the tacking and press the seams open. Now, fold along the seamline so the front and back are positioned with right sides together. Stitch again, but this time 1cm (⅜in) from the fold.

🪡 Try this...

Collars can be tricky to stitch
accurately. This faux collar
makes it easy to add design
detail at the neckline.

4 PREPARE THE SLEEVES

Turn under and press 5mm (¼in), then 1cm (⅜in) to the wrong side along the bottom of one sleeve to form a double hem. Tack, then stitch the hem. Fold the hemmed sleeve in half lengthways and mark the centre of the top of the sleeve with a pin. Repeat with the other sleeve.

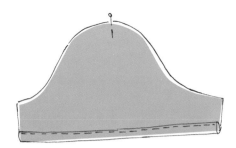

5 SEW ON THE SLEEVES

With wrong sides together, pin one sleeve to the body of the blouse, matching the marker pin with the shoulder seam. Stitch 5mm (¼in) from the edge, then complete the French seam as for the shoulders. Repeat with the other sleeve.

6 STITCH THE SIDE SEAMS

Using the French seam method again, sew the side seams from the bottom edge of the blouse up to the sleeve seam and up the underarm seam – this means stitching the seam first with the wrong sides together (as shown) and then with the right sides together.

7 STITCH THE BLOUSE HEM

Turn up and machine stitch a double hem around the bottom edge of the blouse, folding up 1cm (⅜in) twice to form the hem.

8 ROLL UP THE SLEEVE HEMS

Fold up 1.5cm (⅝in) twice along the hem of one sleeve and press. Make discreet stitches at the armpit and at the outside centre point to hold the fold-up in place. Do the same on the other sleeve.

9 BIND THE NECK EDGE

Starting at the right shoulder, pin and tack the bias binding strip to the neck edge with right sides together. (When you reach the starting point again at the right shoulder, sew the ends of the strip together.) Stitch the binding in place, using a 1.5cm (⅝in) seam allowance. Remove the tacking and trim the seam allowance to 6mm (¼in). Fold under 6mm (¼in) along the edge of the binding, then tack this fold to the wrong side just over the neck seamline. With the right side of the blouse facing you, topstitch along the neck binding close to the seamline – this will catch in the fold on the wrong side. Remove the tacking and press. For a finishing detail, fold the narrow ribbon in half and stitch the fold to the centre front neckline. Trim each length of ribbon to about 30cm (12in) long, cutting on the diagonal, then tie in a bow.

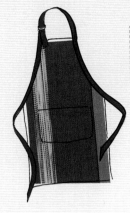

BUTCHER'S APRON

This man's apron is so easy to make, you could easily knock one up in an afternoon and surprise the man in your life with a home-made present.

DIFFICULTY RATING: ⊞ ⊞ ⊞ ⊞ ⊞

Materials

Im (I¼yd) of medium-weight striped fabric II5cm (45in) wide, for apron and pocket

70cm (¾yd) of lightweight denim fabric II5cm (45in) wide, for bias binding

Pair of metal D-loops to fit a 2.5cm- (Iin-) wide neck strap

Matching sewing thread

Back in the 1960s primary school children often cut their sewing teeth on a simple apron. Granted, it was usually a rather more feminine affair than this one – but the principle of making something simple to wear also holds true for this smart but practical butcher's apron.

APRON SIZE
The finished man's apron is 88cm (34¾in) long from the top of the bib to the hemline.

FABRIC FINDER
Butcher's aprons need to protect against splashes and stains, so choose robust fabrics. Choose a lighter weight fabric to make the bias binding.
Try these alternatives for the apron:
Cotton duck—Denim—Medium-weight canvas—Gabardine—Cotton twill
Try these alternatives for the bias binding:
Chambray—Lightweight cotton

SKILLS SET
Working even slipstitch **see page 48**— Stitching double-fold hems **see page 50**
Making and applying bias binding **see pages 70 and 7I**

234

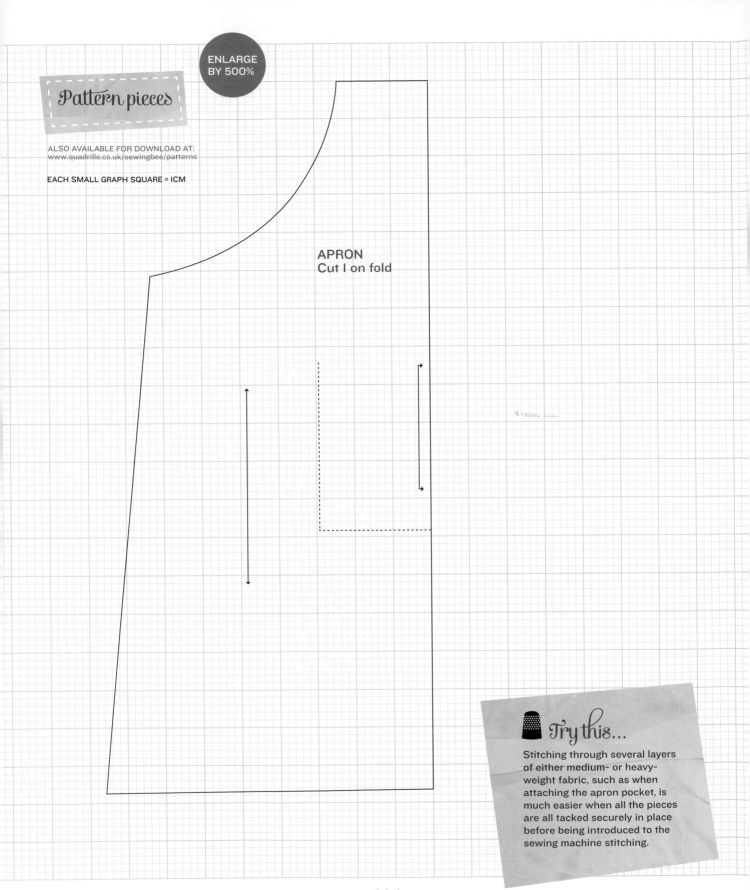

ENLARGE
BY 500%

Pattern pieces

ALSO AVAILABLE FOR DOWNLOAD AT:
www.quadrille.co.uk/sewingbee/patterns

EACH SMALL GRAPH SQUARE = ICM

APRON
Cut I on fold

Try this...

Stitching through several layers
of either medium- or heavy-
weight fabric, such as when
attaching the apron pocket, is
much easier when all the pieces
are all tacked securely in place
before being introduced to the
sewing machine stitching.

Cutting guide

Press the fabrics thoroughly before cutting.

FROM THE STRIPED FABRIC:

✎ Cut one apron piece, on the fold and with the stripes running vertically.

✎ Cut one pocket, measuring 30 x 27cm (11¾ x 10½in), with the stripes running parallel to the longest edge.

FROM THE DENIM FABRIC:

✎ Cut enough 9cm- (3½in-) wide strips on the bias to make a continuous bias binding at least 350cm (138in) long.

To make the apron

1 PREPARE THE POCKET

On the pocket piece, turn 1cm (⅜in) to the wrong side along the bottom edge (parallel to the stripes) and pin; then turn under 1cm (⅜in) along the side edges as well. To mitre the bottom corners to neaten them, fold back the corner at an angle, running between the outer corner and the inner corner where the hems meet. Unfold the pressed hems and the mitre, then snip away the surplus fabric as shown. Refold the corner into position and press again. Tack these hems in place.

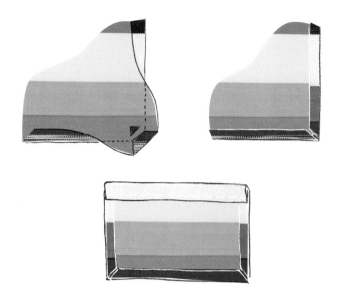

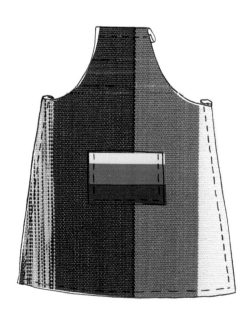

2 HEM THE POCKET

Turn under 2cm (¾in) twice along the top of the pocket to form a double hem and pin. Tack the double hem in place and stitch it close to the first fold. Remove the tacking along the pocket top but keep the tacking in place along the sides and bottom edge. Press the prepared pocket and set it aside.

3 HEM THE APRON EDGES

Turn under 1cm (⅜in) twice along the top of the apron bib. Stitch this double hem in place close to the first fold. Stitch a double hem along the sides and bottom of the apron in the same way, mitring the hemline corners. (Leave the armhole edges raw as these will be bound by the bias binding.) Press.

4 SEW ON THE POCKET

Position the pocket right side up on the front of the apron between the markers and tack. Topstitch the pocket to the apron along three sides, 3mm (⅛in) from the edge. Remove the tacking and press.

5 PREPARE THE BIAS BINDING

Stitch the 9cm- (3½in-) wide bias-cut strips together end to end with 1cm- (⅜in-) wide diagonal seams to produce a continuous strip of binding at least 350cm (138in) long. Fold the strip in half lengthways with the wrong sides together and press. Then open out the strip, fold 2cm (¾in) toward the centre along each long edge and press. Now refold it along the centre and press again for a 2.5cm (1in) folded binding width. Cut the strip into two lengths with squared ends – one 187cm (73½in) long and one 142cm (56in) long. Turn 1cm (⅜in) to the inside along each short end of each of these binding pieces and pin these hems in place.

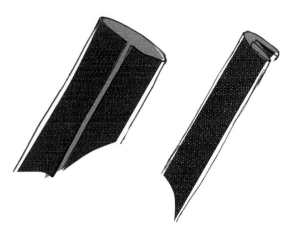

6 STITCH ON THE BINDING

With the apron right side up, pin the longest strip of prepared binding to the armhole on the right-hand side of the apron. To do this, leave 85cm (33½in) of the binding free at the bottom of the armhole for the waist tie and then pin the binding evenly along the armhole with the apron sandwiched inside the binding – this leaves about 65cm (25½in) free at the bib end for the neck strap. Pin the shorter binding strip to the other side of the apron in the same way, again leaving 85cm (33½in) free for the waist tie – this leaves about 20cm (8in) free at the bib end for the neck strap. Tack the entire length of each binding strip together along the folds, catching in the apron where the strips are pinned to the armhole. Topstitch the binding 3mm (⅛in) from the edge, including along the waist tie, armhole, neck strap and the turned under short ends. Remove the tacking and press the binding.

7 SEW ON THE D-LOOPS

Thread a pair of metal D-loops onto the end of the longest neck strap, fold 7cm (2¾in) of the strap to the wrong side and slipstitch the last 2cm (¾in) in place. Lace the short neck strap onto the D-loops ready to be adjusted.

Try this…

If you find making bias binding a
bit of a fiddle, check out your local
haberdashers for a bias binding
maker. It's a small metal handtool
that makes quick work of all the
folding. They come in many sizes,
though a good standard size bias
is 6cm (2½in) cut but not folded.

RUFFLE CUSHION

This cushion is modern yet fun, kept smart by teaming a neutral pleated grosgrain trim with the bold main colour.

DIFFICULTY RATING: ●● ●● ●● ●● ●●

Cushions are great beginner projects. They don't demand too much fabric and are essentially just two squares or rectangles stitched together, yet they can be surprisingly expensive to buy. By stitching your own, you can afford to use the very best fabrics and trimmings, to quickly, easily and inexpensively bring a whole new look to your interior. If you're going to make your own cushions, it's always lovely to add your own creative touches with frills, trims or piping. Most are stitched into the seams of the cushion – and the pleated ribbon on this one demonstrates the basic method. If you don't feel ready to put in a zip (which is a little trickier than simple straight sewing), then slipstitch the cover to enclose the cushion pad and when it comes to laundering, just undo the slipstitching, wash and re-slipstitch to close up again.

CUSHION SIZE
Excluding the ruffles, the finished cushion measures 50 x 30cm (19¾ x 11¾in).

FABRIC FINDER
Scatter cushions like this, can be made and trimmed with almost any fabric, including dress fabrics, though furnishing fabrics are more hard-wearing. A closely woven, medium- to heavy-weight wool fabric like this is great for cushions as it resists stains and doesn't crease.
Try these as alternatives:
Cotton—Silk—Linen—Brocade

Materials
40cm (½yd) of a medium- to heavy-weight closely woven fabric at least 115cm (45in) wide
1.4m (1½yd) of striped grosgrain ribbon 4cm (1½in) wide
Matching invisible zip 50cm (20in) long
Matching sewing thread
Cushion pad 50 x 30cm (19¾ x 11¾in), to fit finished cover

SKILLS SET
Stitching straight seams **see page 51**—Finishing seams **see pages 54 and 55**
Inserting an invisible zip **see pages 68 and 69**

Cutting guide

Press the fabric thoroughly before cutting.

FROM THE FABRIC:

✂ Cut two pieces of fabric, each 52 x 32cm (20¾ x 12¾in).

FROM THE GROSGRAIN RIBBON:

✂ Cut the length of ribbon into two equal lengths.

The 1cm (½in) seam allowance is included on the fabric pieces.

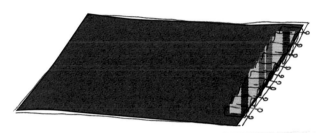

2 INSERT THE INVISIBLE ZIP

Insert the invisible zip along one long edge between the two cushion cover pieces, making sure it is centred with 3cm (1¼in) allowance at either end. Take a 1cm (½in) seam allowance when inserting the zip.

3 STITCH THE COVER TOGETHER

Open the zip, then pin the two cover pieces with right sides together. With the piece with the ruffle stitching line facing upwards and starting at one end of the zip, stitch the two layers together, taking a 1cm (½in) seam allowance and ending at the other end of the zip. Stitch just outside the ruffle stitching so it won't show when you turn the cover right side out. Also, take care not to catch the side of the ruffle into the seam. Trim off a triangle of fabric at each of the corners. Turn the cover right side out, pushing out the corners using a knitting needle or any other blunt point. Press firmly. Insert the cushion pad and zip up.

To make the ruffle cushion

1 PLEAT AND ADD THE RUFFLES

Take your time over this stage and aim for precise, even pleats. First, lay the cushion piece wrong side down on a flat surface. Turn under 1cm (½in) twice along one short end of the grosgrain to make a double hem and, with right sides together, pin this end to one short edge of the cushion piece, placing it 1.5cm (⅝in) from the end to allow room for the seam allowance. Make even pleats, pinning them to the edge of the fabric as you go and finishing 1.5cm (⅝in) from the end. Viewed from the right side, each of these pleats should be 3cm (1³⁄₁₆in) wide, and have a return of about 1.5cm (⅝in). You should end up with ten pleats 3cm (1³⁄₁₆in) apart. At the end of the ruffle turn under a 1cm (½in) double hem again. Stitch the grosgrain to the fabric piece using a 1cm (½in) seam allowance. Stitch the grosgrain to the other end of the cushion in the same way, ensuring the pleats lie in the same direction as they do on the other side of the cushion.

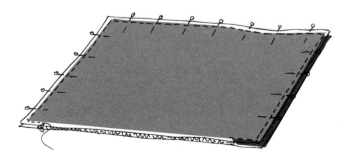

SEWING GLOSSARY

BASTING Another word for **TACKING**.

BIAS On fabric, this runs diagonally across the grain at 45 degrees to the selvedge. This is where you can get most stretch out of the fabric. See also **GRAIN**.

BIAS BINDING Binding that is made from fabric cut on the bias.

BODICE The top part of a dress from the neckline to where it is sewn into the skirt.

CASING A channel created for threading through elastic or cord when making drawstring items.

DART A fold (often triangular or diamond-shaped) sewn into the cut-out fabric to give the garment a three-dimensional shape to fit the contours of the body.

FACINGS These are small pieces, cut to the same shape as an edge such as a neckline. Once sewn into position, they are folded to the inside to create a neat outside edge.

FINISHING Ways of neatening the raw edges on the inside of seams (see pages 50–51).

FRAYING The unravelling of raw edges.

GRAIN The threads in the fabric running either horizontally or vertically. Straight of grain, or lengthwise grain, runs parallel with the selvedge and does not have any stretch. Cross grain or crosswise grain, runs between the selvedges and stretches slightly, but is also a 'straight grain'. See also **BIAS**.

GUSSET A piece of fabric used to create the three-dimensional element of some items such as the sides and bottom of a bag, the crotch of underwear, or even a small triangle of fabric at the end of a shirt seam.

HEM A neat finish whereby raw edges are turned to the inside of the garment. A double hem is folded over twice to enclose the raw edge on the inside before sewing, eliminating any fraying or unravelling.

INTERFACING Fabric used between the main garment piece and the facing to provide stabilisation and extra body to the garment. Cut to the same size and shape as the facing, these were traditionally tacked into place. Nowadays, specialised interfacings can be fused into position using a hot iron.

INTERLINING A layer between the main fabric and lining used to add body and warmth to curtains.

NAP This is the pile element on fabrics such as velvet, corduroy, velour, velveteen that is woven into the material during the construction process.

PINTUCKS Tiny tucks, often stitched in parallel groups used to add detail.

RAW EDGES Any fabric edge other than a selvedge.

RIGHT SIDES TOGETHER When sewing seams, fabric is placed so that the right side of the front piece is laid on top of the right side of the back piece with the shapes matching ready for sewing. See also **WRONG SIDES TOGETHER**.

SELVEDGES These are the finished edges running down either side of the fabric. They do not fray or unravel.

STAY STITCHING Straight machine stitching worked just inside a seam allowance to strengthen it and prevent it from stretching or breaking.

TACKING Long temporary hand stitches used to hold pieces of fabric together before and during the machine stitching or final stitching step.

THROAT PLATE The metal plate on the sewing machine underneath the needle and presser foot. It incorporates a hole for the needle and the feed dogs, which are metal teeth-like ridges that move the fabric forward as you sew.

TOPSTITCHING A line of stitches used decoratively to finish off the outside of a seam.

WRONG SIDES TOGETHER This is the term used when the wrong side of one piece is laid on top of the wrong side of another piece before sewing.

YOKE This is an extra piece of fabric at the top of a shirt or skirt to create an extra design element or extra strength. It is sometimes cut on the bias to emphasise the design.

FABRIC DICTIONARY

ACETATE
A silky synthetic fabric with excellent draping qualities. Most commonly used for garment linings.

BATIK
Printed cotton designs indigenous to Indonesia and Java. Wax is applied to the parts of the fabric that are to be left uncoloured. The fabric is then dyed and once fully dried, boiled to remove the wax. This is repeated for each colour, building up the design layer by layer.

BOUCLÉ
A woolly fabric incorporating loops and curls for a 'poodle' effect.

BROCADE
Richly patterned fabric with the design incorporated into the weave. Woven by hand for centuries in China, an extra horizontal thread is carried across the wrong side, which means the fabric is not reversible in contrast to damask, which is similar but fully reversible.

CALICO
Inexpensive, plain-woven, unbleached cotton fabric. Available in its natural state, it was previously offered as brightly patterned fabric known as calico prints.

CANVAS
A firmly woven heavy-weight cotton.

CASHMERE
An expensive wool fibre made from Kashmiri goat hair. Very fine, soft and warm.

CHALLIS
This is a soft, lightweight, often printed, fabric, traditionally woven from wool.

CHAMBRAY
A soft cotton fabric where the vertical threads are coloured and the horizontal, white.

CHIFFON
This fine, sheer fabric was traditionally made from silk. Nowadays, you also see synthetic chiffon.

CHINO
A twill-woven cotton that has been 'mercerised' to increase its strength and lustre.

CHINTZ
A crisp, densely woven glazed cotton. Traditionally, it was printed (hence the word, chintzy).

CORDUROY
A cotton fabric featuring cut pile ridges. Available in several sizes from fine (needle) to large (elephant).

COTTON DUCK
Heavy-weight canvas-like cotton, woven using a single horizontal thread over and under pairs of vertical threads. It comes in twelve weights ranging from the heaviest, Number 1 (18oz) for hammocks, to Number 12 (7oz), for lightweight clothes.

CREPE
Any fabric that incorporates twisted fibres to give a crinkled surface and improve drape.

CREPE DE CHINE
This is a silky crepe fabric where both vertical and horizontal threads are twisted before weaving.

DAMASK
A rich pattern-woven fabric similar to brocade. The difference is that damask is fully reversible.

DENIM
Robust cotton originating from Nimes in France (de Nimes, shortened to denim). The traditionally blue vertical threads are twill woven with white horizontals.

DOBBY
Fabrics featuring all-over woven repeats, which can take the form of a texture or a coloured pattern. They're woven using a special head on a Jacquard-type loom.

DOGTOOTH CHECK
A pointed, star-like twill weave design using two contrasting colours. Larger versions are called houndstooth and smaller ones, puppy tooth.

DUPION
A dense, slubby (knobbly) silk fabric woven from fibres reeled off two cocoons. Synthetic versions, woven from synthetic slubby yarns, are now available.

ELASTANE
The generic name for Lycra.

FABRIC DYED
Fabric that has been woven, before being dyed, for a soft, washed, slightly faded look as the colour doesn't penetrate the fibres quite so efficiently.

FLANNEL
A soft plain- or twill-woven cotton or wool.

GABARDINE
Tightly woven twill with a slight sheen.

GARMENT DYED
The fabric is dyed before the garment is made up for a washed look highlighting seams and turnings where the dye hasn't fully penetrated.

GEORGETTE
Similar to chiffon but heavier, this is a plain-weave crepe, traditionally made from silk.

GINGHAM
This firmly woven cotton is best known for its characteristic woven checked design in different sizes.

GROSGRAIN
A ribbon with distinctive ribs. Strong cotton horizontal threads are woven through fine silk or rayon.

IKAT
An ancient decorative fabric form with distinctive designs created by tying fibres into bundles using waxed threads so they can be part dyed before weaving.

INTERLOCK
A fine cotton knit traditionally used for underwear, this is now also used for outerwear.

JACQUARD
An elaborate loom invented in 1802 by Joseph Marie Jacquard to mechanise the production of brocades and damasks. Since its invention, any pattern-woven fabric or ribbon is generally referred to as 'a Jacquard'.

JERSEY
The name for knitted fabrics. T-shirt material is made from cotton jersey.

KNITTED FABRICS
All jerseys are created using a form of knit. This produces a soft, fluid fabric with plenty of stretch, even if it's made totally of natural fibres.

LAMÉ
Any fabric woven through with metallic threads.

LYCRA
A brand name for spandex, an extremely stretchy fibre.

MADRAS
A plain-woven, lightweight cotton from India that is characterised by striped and checked designs.

MOIRÉ
A watery effect created on ribbed fabric using steam, heat and chemicals.

NYLON
The trade name for polyamide, an original synthetic fabric. It's mixed with other fibres for added strength.

ORGANDIE
This sheer cotton fabric has a crisp quality that survives laundering, created by tightly twisting the yarns before weaving them together.

ORGANZA A silk organdie. Often made from soft, sheer synthetics, which lack the characteristic crisp drape.

OXFORD
A cotton basket-weave fabric, created by using two horizontal threads to weave under and over the verticals two at a time. Often used for casual shirts.

PAISLEY
A curved, teardrop-style motif native to the Indian sub-continent. It is named after the Scottish town of Paisley, where it is printed onto fine wool (challis).

PIQUE
This dobby woven cotton with its raised geometric design is a popular choice for casual wear, because it is cool, comfortable and resists creases.

POPLIN
A fine (usually) cotton weave with a subtle rib running across its width.

POLYESTER
A versatile synthetic, often used in combination with natural fabrics.

RAW SILK
Natural, undyed silk before the gum has been removed. When woven, it gives a slubbed effect.

RAYON
One of the first synthetic fibres, first produced in 1891 as an alternative to silk.

SATEEN
A variation of the satin weave, created by carrying the horizontal threads over several vertical threads and then under one, giving a softer sheen than satin.

SATIN WEAVE
To create a sheen on one side of the fabric, the horizontal threads (weft) go under several vertical threads (warp), and over just one, then under several again. It's most effective and easily created using long fibres that have their own sheen, such as silk, but any fibre can be woven into a satin weave.

SEERSUCKER
A finely woven partly crinkled cotton. The name comes from the Anglicised Hindustani word for milk and sugar, describing the smooth/crinkled texture.

SHANTUNG
Originally a slubbed (knobbly) silk, it now also describes synthetic slubbed fabrics.

SHOT SILK
By weaving together horizontal (weft) threads of one colour with vertical (warp) threads in a different colour, the fabric takes on an iridescent effect.

SLUB
A slubbed yarn is uneven or knobbly along its length. When woven, it creates a slubbed fabric.

SPANDEX
Also known as Elastane or Lycra, spandex is a supremely stretchy synthetic developed in the 1950s. Originally used for swimwear, it is now also mixed with natural fibres to keep the fabrics in shape.

TAFFETA
A crisp fabric with a slight sheen, made from silk, rayon or nylon.

TAPESTRY
A heavy embroidered fabric in which the horizontal threads completely cover the vertical. When it is machine made, the pattern is woven in using extra horizontal threads in a similar way to brocade.

TARTAN
A range of twill-woven wool plaids from Scotland.

TICKING
A densely woven striped cotton twill originally designed for mattresses. The quality of the smartly striped cloth has made it a popular furnishing fabric.

TOILE DE JOUY
Originated from Jouy-en-Josas in the late eighteenth century, the printed designs on usually cream cotton depict delightful pastoral scenes.

TULLE
Machine-made fine netting that was originally silk, but is now more often polyester.

TUSSAH
Made from silk from abandoned cocoons of India's wild silk worms, this fibre has a natural slub.

TWEED
Slubby, flecked woollen fabric.

TWILL
A robust weave with a diagonal 'rib'. The twill most of us know best is denim, though chinos, drill, tartan, houndstooth and ticking are also examples of twill. Twill is created by weaving the horizontal threads (weft) over two vertical threads (warp) and under one. The resulting fabric is hard-wearing, naturally resists soiling and has a wonderful drape. Herringbone is a variant.

VELOUR
A soft fabric with a short thick (usually cotton) pile, although it can also be seen in wool or mohair.

VELVET
This luxurious pile fabric was traditionally made from silk; nowadays, it is more likely to be synthetic.

VISCOSE
A type of rayon, a silky synthetic fibre.

VOILE
Made from twisted yarns woven in a plain weave, this is a crisp semi sheer.

WOOLLEN
A bulky fabric made from wool that has been carded but not combed before being woven, so that it retains some of the characteristic shorter fibres.

WORSTED
A fine-quality wool fabric that has been both carded and combed before being spun into strong fine yarns and then closely woven for a smooth, crisp fabric.

INDEX

ACKNOWLEDGEMENTS

LOVE PRODUCTIONS would like to thank everyone involved in the series and book of 'The Great British Sewing Bee': the brilliant team at Quadrille Publishing and Tessa Evelegh for producing such a beautiful book; Sewing Bee judges May Martin and Patrick Grant, host Claudia Winkleman, the dedicated production team and crew for making a great series and Amanda Console for promoting it; Janice Hadlow, Alison Kirkham and Emma Willis at the BBC for commissioning us. And most of all our sewers – Ann, Jane, Lauren, Mark, Michelle, Sandra, Stuart and Tilly – you have been an inspiration.

TESSA EVELEGH would like to thank the team that has put The Great British Sewing Bee book together...

Stephanie Boissard for her inspired fashion designs and hard work to get everything done on time.

Jeanne Laine for her fabulous home furnishing and accessory designs.

Annie Kelley (Annie2Pins) for her brilliant stitching of the sewing skills.

Claire Louise Hardie (CL) for providing sewers at such short notice.

Lizzie Moul and her helpers, *Francis Campbell* and *Maria Liljefors* for sewing a garments in a weekend.

Tilly Walnes of Tilly and the Buttons for generously sharing her pattern with us.

To all at *Love Productions*, including *Anna Beattie* for her unerring judgement, *Catherine Lewendon* for getting me involved, *Letty Kavanagh* for her firm hand on the tiller, *May Martin* for checking the instructions and generally being lovely, *Patrick Grant* for his sheer style, *James Morgan* for his creativity and calm, *Jane Treasure* for supplying the programme information for the book, *Susanne Rock* for her diplomacy and care and attention to the book, and the production team, *Addy*, *Steve* and *Sophie*, who looked after everyone's needs. *Stuart Cooper* at MetroStar for getting the book team together.

To all at *Quadrille Publishing* including, *Jane O'Shea* for her wisdom, taste and sharp eye for a deadline, *Claire Peters* for making the book beautiful, *Helen Lewis* for overseeing the look of the book and *Lisa Pendreigh* for her cool-headed clarity in steering the book and to *Sally Harding* for her dedication in editing the instructions.

To the photography team, including *Laura Edwards* for her evocative photographs and *Jazmine Rocks* for her inspired, refreshing styling.

QUADRILLE PUBLISHING would like to thank the following:
Designers Guild, Kahaila Cafe, Labour and Wait, Malabar, Osborne & Little, Paul Johnston at *Fabrics Galore, Singer Sewing Machines, The Linen Works, Vanessa Arbuthnott, Warren and Sharon* at *Wimbledon Sewing Machine Shop, Tara Starlet, Bertie, Dune* and *Pied a Terre.*

This book is published to accompany the television series entitled *The Great British Sewing Bee*, first broadcast on BBC TWO in 2013.

Executive Producer Anna Beattie
Series Editor Susanne Rock
Series Director James Morgan
Senior Producers Catherine Lewendon, Jane Treasure
Sewing Consultant Claire Louise Hardie,
The Thrifty Stitcher
Head of Production Leatty Kavanagh
BBC Commissioning Executive Emma Willis

This edition was first published in 2013 by
Quadrille Publishing Ltd
www.quadrille.co.uk

Text © Love Productions 2013
Project designs © Love Productions 2013 with the exception of
page 90–95: Mathilde Blouse © Tilly Walnes
page 112–119: Simplicity 2886 © Simplicity Ltd
page 170–177: New Look 6035 © Simplicity Ltd

Photography © Laura Edwards 2013
Design, illustrations and layout © Quadrille Publishing Ltd 2013

British Library Cataloguing-in-Publication Data
A catalogue record for this book is available from the British Library.

Reprinted in 2014
10 9 8 7 6 5 4 3 2

ISBN 978 184949 462 5

Quadrille craft

Publishing Director Jane O'Shea
Commissioning Editor Lisa Pendreigh
Copy Editors Sally Harding and Sarah Hoggett
Creative Director Helen Lewis
Art Direction & Design Claire Peters
Designers Nicola Ellis and Gemma Hogan
Photographer Laura Edwards
Stylist Jazmine Rocks
Stylist's Asisstants Marianna Frannais
  and Becky O'Riordan
Hair & Make-up Danielle Hooker
Models Iskra and Quita at Hughes, Josephine at BMA,
  Sarah at Close, Tony at M&P, Honey at Bruce & Brown
  and Chinh
Illustrators Bridget Bodoano, Joy FitzSimmons
  and Claire Peters
Production Director Vincent Smith
Production Controller Sasha Taylor

Printed and bound in China.

If you have any comments or queries regarding the instructions in this book, please contact us at enquiries@quadrille.co.uk.